Character is free and costs the busir
ing, but if you don't have character, it
everything. Compassion for others and
succeed will flourish the entire company. Leaders with character understand that you sometimes lead from the front, and sometimes you must lead from the rear. The sense of humanity must be shared with all who are involved.

—Coach Joseph Taylor
Vice President of Intercollegiate Athletics,
Virginia Union University,
College Football Hall of Fame (2019),
and Black College Football Hall of Fame (2020)

Jonathan, I am blessed beyond measure to call you friend. What a joy it has been to witness the growth and success of Easy Step Enterprises. The entire team's passion for changing lives through transformational products is contagious! Jonathan and his teams have seen massive growth by caring and investing deeply in the development of their people, creating a culture based on integrity and character. The best is yet to come!

—Chad Johnson
Chief Inspiration Officer for The Giant 5 Guy

Many years ago, Jonathan adopted TAPS as a cause he was passionate about. He understood service and sacrifice and knew how precious and precarious our freedoms are. Jonathan has become part of our extended TAPS family, and we know he stands with us because he has had personal pain and grief in his own life and has now turned that compassion into action for others.

—Bonnie Carroll
President and Founder of the Tragedy Assistance
Program for Survivors (TAPS)

THE BUSINESS OF
CHARACTER

Accelerate Business Growth with Vibrant Culture and Intentional Character

THE BUSINESS OF
CHARACTER

Accelerate Business Growth with Vibrant Culture and Intentional Character

JONATHAN COTTEN

ethos
collective

Published by Igniting Souls
PO Box 43, Powell, OH 43065
IgnitingSouls.com

LCCN: 2024923788
Paperback ISBN: 978-1-63680-424-8
Hardcover ISBN: 978-1-63680-425-5
e-book ISBN: 978-1-63680-426-2

Available in paperback, hardcover, e-book, and audiobook.

Dedication

So many times, I looked around and felt hopeless. Then, I looked inward and felt helpless. Only when I looked up to you, Lord, did I find amazing grace, confidence, and courage. Thank you for loving me, for blessing me with my wife Kathryn, for my children Joseph, Jarrin, Jennings, Jentry, and Kayla, and for my grandchildren, Grayson, Kipling, Reagan, Jude, Kensi, Remington, Beckley, Whitfield, Winston, Lincoln, Mina, June, and Koa. "The blessing of the Lord makes a person rich, and he adds no sorrow with it" (Proverbs 10:22, NKJV). Thank you also to all who have contributed in ways large and small both to Easy Step Enterprises and this book. You have truly made it a joy to be in The Business of Character.

Table of Contents

A business, successful or not, is merely a reflection of the character of its leadership.

—S. Truett Cathy, Founder of Chick-fil-A

Foreword by Wayne Jacobson

There's nothing more I treasure in a friend than genuineness.

I don't look for perfection; we all have blind spots and weaknesses. People don't have to be successful, humorous, or well-connected. I want them to be real—to enjoy what they enjoy, be vulnerable to struggle where they struggle, and be curious to question what they need to question while respecting the same process in others. Openness and honesty are crucial to sharing a healthy friendship.

I don't like finding out later that people told me what they thought I wanted to hear, whether to protect my feelings or save them from a difficult conversation. Duplicity is unbecoming of anyone. Those who flatter or fawn only serve themselves at another's expense. I'll take an honest challenge over a disingenuous compliment any day of the week.

For me, genuineness is even more important when someone puts thoughts to paper for others to consider. I've met too many writers who don't live up to the image they project in their writings or aspire to the ideals they put before others. Words are empty if they are not backed by a life that reflects them.

That's why Jonathan Cotten is my kind of human.

I've had many opportunities to be with Jonathan in a variety of settings, including in his home, to see the care he has for family and friends. I have benefited from his kindness and generosity, and I know many others have as well.

I've been with him on the job to see how he deals with employees and customers alike. There is no better measure of a man's character than how he treats the people around him. Is he out to gain an advantage at another's expense or looking for a fair exchange for both parties?

I've also wandered around his city with him, engaging marginalized groups in his community. I've seen his compassionate heart and ability to engage in meaningful conversations with diverse people.

And I've watched him struggle through excruciating crises, especially with those he loves, as he endures the dark night of the soul where he carries more questions than answers. I've watched him make choices of conscience, sometimes against his own self-interest for the benefit of others. I've seen him struggle with difficult decisions that tested his character and his compassion for others and prevailed in doing what was right, not personally expedient.

So, more than recommending his thoughts to you, let me commend the man himself. He's as genuine a man as I've been pleased to know. His compass is locked on a purpose greater than himself that informs his actions and graciousness to others.

As he shares what he has learned, you can rest assured that he speaks from a reservoir of wisdom gained through personal experience. His business acumen is enriching, his passion for life contagious, his business ethics exemplary, and his faith deep and abiding.

These are the words of a man who means them. I trust they will enrich and inspire you as much as his life has touched me.

—Wayne Jacobsen
Author of *He Loves Me* and *So You Don't
Want to Go to Church Anymore*
and Co-Author of *The Shack*

Introduction
The Crucible of Character

The Turning Point: Adversity at Midlife

For we walk by faith, not by sight.
—*2 Corinthians 5:7 (NKJV)*

In my late 40s, I was experiencing what many might describe as a midlife crisis. I don't know that it was as much of an age thing as it was a convergence—or collision might be a better word—of concerns about my faith as a Christian, the health of a loved one, and finding significant purpose in life. It all started with running, an activity I had become more devoted to as I got older.

I first took up running as a discipline, like eating your spinach. I would put on my running shoes, go out for a couple of miles, come back home, and cross it off the checklist. I did not enjoy it, but it got done.

When I began to extend my runs in my early 40s to distances of three to five miles, they became something else. They were my time alone to think, pray, and process things. Like running, life can have painful, lonely stretches. My running routine helped me maintain balance as I experienced challenges, which inevitably come for us all to one degree or another. Unfortunately, as I extended my running distance, by the end of 2011, I developed plantar fasciitis, an inflammatory condition of the tissue in my feet, bringing my progress to a halt.

Though I tried to persevere, my pain was significant and forced me to go on shorter runs of only a mile or two. I was extremely worried that without help, I would have to stop running completely, leaving me without a much-needed way to let off steam. Immediately, I started searching for a solution: I rolled my feet on tennis balls. I bought some new shoes. I tried all the over-the-counter cushions and insoles from the drugstores and big box retail stores, and I saw a doctor who suggested stretching exercises. But nothing helped. My condition got worse, affecting more than my running. Soon, I even had to hobble to the bathroom in the morning as if I were a much older man.

In January 2012, I was close to giving up when I remembered I had heard about The Good Feet Store in Richmond, Virginia. I knew their products were not the cheap solutions I had already tried, but I had nothing left to lose. I visited the store one day and got fitted for arch supports by the friendly and professional staff there. I started running again with the arch supports in, and sure enough, in about two weeks, the pain in my heels and Achilles tendons was gone. Running was suddenly fun again—which was good, considering the impending storm my family, particularly my daughter Kayla, was about to face.

As the youngest child with older brothers, Kayla always wanted to keep up with the boys. Whether it was watching them play basketball or trying to eat as much as they could at mealtimes, her brothers were the pacesetters, and she was determined to stay right there with them. In November 2011, Kayla contracted Norovirus, which made her violently ill for a few days. Though she initially seemed to have recovered, my wife, Kathryn, and I noticed that Kayla would have mild but ongoing relapses with some of the same symptoms as if the virus never entirely left and still had a hold on her immune system. Her appetite got worse as well. In early 2012, she started losing weight; by March, her condition was even worse, and Kathryn and I took her to the hospital for the first time.

The doctors ran tests but couldn't precisely identify what was wrong. Unable to help, they sent us home. This process repeated for the next six weeks, with our family taking six more visits to the ER. We were still scrambling for a way to help our daughter, and when I wasn't doing at-home medical research or taking care of Kayla, I was focusing on my job and on running to keep myself on an even keel.

In May, I was on a business trip in Rhode Island when Kathryn called me from the hospital with news from the ER doctors. Kayla's condition had worsened again: she was severely malnourished and would have to be hospitalized to receive artificial nutrition. After multiple weeks in the hospital, Kayla finally got her diagnosis. She had mitochondrial disease, and it was causing gastroparesis and other conditions.

Simultaneously, I encountered another significant challenge that went to the core of my being and impacted my priorities and worldview. Faith has been at the center of my life since childhood. I was raised in a loving family with a mom and dad who were devoted Christians and taught me many truths from the Bible. On June 11, 1979, I knelt beside my bed and asked Jesus to save me. That was an authentic moment, consistent with the words in Romans 10:9: "If you declare with your mouth, 'Jesus is Lord,' and believe in your heart that God raised him from the dead, you will be saved."

Yet we were part of a multi-generational fellowship that, over the years, had developed an authoritarian, rules-based structure. At the same time, it was a highly connected social network, with many healthy relationships on both individual and familial levels. Our calendar revolved around Bible studies, retreats, and recreational activities, with limited engagement outside these circles. This was everyday life, and the fellowship's mission was to build healthy families centered around the Bible as a response to a culture that seemed increasingly unmoored from those values.

Kayla's sickness interrupted this schedule and lifestyle. I had already begun to question whether our fellowship truly embraced the message of grace that is the essence of the Gospel of Jesus Christ. Now, as I wrestled with Kayla's health journey, those questions were top of mind. A Christian resolves the most profound challenges through a personal relationship with God and not through another person or a religious system. That was what I began to experience more and more.

To maintain my physical, emotional, and spiritual balance at the time, I kept increasing my running distances until September 2012, when I decided to tackle my first marathon—even though it was only about six weeks away. While that training preparation is not advisable, it worked well enough in my case, and in November 2012, I crossed the finish line at the Richmond Marathon.

In the summer of 2013, Kayla was able to get a gastric pacemaker, which involved a month-long stay at Nationwide Children's Hospital in Columbus, Ohio. Once again, Kayla endured twists and turns like battling her fourth sepsis infection. My family was blessed that my then-employer, Plus Relocation Services, was so accommodating throughout our ordeal; they allowed me to take conference calls and work from my laptop, which I did in Kayla's hospital room or the family waiting room. Through her care and high emotional intelligence, Susan Benevides, the President of Plus Relocation, set a great example for me of what a culture of authentic care for employees really looks like.

After so much time in the hospital, I gained a new appreciation for medical professionals from the nurses who cared for my daughter. Kayla's nurses were and still are true wonder workers, as are many of her doctors. Even so, there were times when we had to challenge the doctor's authority in a direct, unyielding way.

In these moments of challenges with doctors, I felt parallels to the challenges others had made in the past, and to the religious practices of our fellowship. I had defended those practices because it had been a lifetime perspective, yet now the realization shook me to the core; I had been wrong on issues that were the most critical and high-priority beliefs and values. Not only was I wrong, but consistent with my personality, I influenced others with misguided zeal. I tried to sort out a lifetime belief structure and keep up with the demands of my job while advocating for Kayla's care in our complicated healthcare system; it all took its toll. I kept running—with the help of my life-saving arch supports—and in addition to helping me feel like I was still sane, I hashed out life with God.

One Saturday afternoon in September 2013, Kayla and I were on our way to get her first cell phone before she returned to school after an 18-month hiatus due to her health struggles. The store was about 20 minutes from our home in Montpelier, Virginia, and as we were driving down Broad Street, I remembered that I'd wanted to visit The Good Feet Store again. I needed to buy cushions to go with my arch supports to help me for my second marathon (which, like the first time, was now just six weeks away). Now, my training regimen was more structured, making running more enjoyable.

It was the first time I'd been back to the store since getting my arch supports, and as we walked in that day, I approached the owner, Mary, with a heart full of gratitude.

"I've never bought a product that has transformed my life like these arch supports have," I told her. Mary was helping another customer, and as she walked across the sales floor, she pivoted, turning back to look at me.

"You wanna buy the place?" she asked. At first, I just laughed because her question took me by surprise. But something in her words made me realize this wasn't just a passing comment.

Kayla and I left, but I kept thinking about Mary's offer the whole way home. When I told my wife, Kathryn, what happened, she could sense my enthusiasm for the idea was growing.

"Maybe you should check it out," she said with a shrug. Once again, I was taken aback. I knew my wife to be an extremely risk-averse person, so for her, that was an incredibly bold statement. It was only the second time I could remember her deviating from her usual conservative approach. The first was when she said yes to marrying 19-year-old me, who only had $150 or so in his bank account and was working on commission.

That day, she gave me the green light to leave a secure and profitable job in the relocation industry, where I had worked for over 25 years, to consider owning a store I knew virtually nothing about. It was a risk on steroids.

Encouraged by my wife, I returned to the store a week later.

"Mary," I asked, "Were you really serious about wanting to sell the store?"

"Yes," she responded, "I am not cut out to be an owner."

I took a moment before I could respond. "Well, go ahead and put your numbers together, and let's talk."

After reviewing Mary's profit and loss statement, I realized that the primary issues to be solved were sales and marketing challenges, which were areas of business I was most confident about. Knowing how the arch supports helped me, I believed there was a large market for others with similar needs. Within a few weeks, we'd made a deal. I was in the process of detaching from a toxic, lifelong fellowship, and we were still running an emotionally exhausting health journey with Kayla, so I did what any reasonable person would do. I resigned from my job, leaving behind a 25-plus-year career. On January 2, 2014, I began my entrepreneurial journey in an industry I had no experience in, with a concept I knew very little about other than as a satisfied customer. But I was now the owner of The Good Feet Store in Richmond, Virginia.

The transition wasn't easy, and it took more time, money, and effort than I had anticipated, but it turned out that my wife and I had been right. With the help of some outstanding employees, I could do it—and over the last 10 years, our annual revenue has increased by an average of 58 percent per year, with 42 locations from Cleveland, Ohio, to Destin, Florida. I am thankful for that success as well as for the tremendous help and support from friends, family, and coworkers along the way.

All of these experiences have forced me to answer a handful of questions with increasing frequency:

How did I do this?

How did I start with one store, one other employee, and not much money?

What was my business plan?

What was my experience?

How did I finance it?

Answering those questions once and for all is part of the purpose of this book. The other part is to share some of our underlying principles and values that have generated those results. Hopefully, by reading my story and the journey of my business, you will feel motivated and encouraged that you, too, can create a thriving culture and a company with very intentional character.

I also hope to offer new business owners, leaders, and those going through complex transitions of their own more than just the systems and decisions my team and I used to grow our business. More importantly than the store count and revenue growth, I want to offer the deeper values and frameworks behind those systems and decisions from someone who has struggled through them and found success.

While it will take the entire book to explain these things in depth, I'll first save you a little time upfront by answering them briefly:

How did I do this? One day at a time, by the grace of God and not on my strength alone.

How did I start with one store, one other employee, and not much money? I believed to the core in the viability of Good Feet arch supports and their ability to change people's lives as they had changed mine. I knew this business would draw others to it, and more employees and a steady revenue stream would hopefully result from those changed lives.

What was my business plan? There wasn't a real business plan at the beginning.

What was my experience? I had never owned a retail store before. Even without extensive business school training, I did have more than 25 years of experience observing companies of various sizes implement different strategies with employees and customers. I also saw how those strategies affected everyone involved with the organization. Although I didn't have a formal written business plan, I was always eager to learn about and observe leading companies' practices. Now was the chance to implement those observations and the principles I had adopted. A fire was burning within me to test these in the marketplace and see the response from employees, customers, and the community.

How did I finance it? Banks and lenders would not give me the time of day. We started our business on a shoestring as it relates to financing. To come up with the $107,000 purchase price, we took a home equity line advance and raided our 401K, plus a very modest amount for an operating account (a balance of less than $10,000, which is not much cushion). Such an approach demands immediate focus on quickly bringing money in and being profitable. It is a risky approach to business and not really advisable, but it does force you to focus and create a drive for results.

If you primarily measure business success in financial terms, this book may not be for you. Other stories are far more impressive from a growth or financial perspective. It is, on the other hand, for anyone with mission and purpose as primary motivators and the drive to harness the business's power to dramatically change the lives of employees, customers, and members of the surrounding community. This has been my experience with Easy Step Enterprises, and it has been a blessing.

The CEO always gets disproportionate credit for an organization's success, and I am no exception. As excited and passionate as I was about this opportunity, the results would have been minimal if it had continued to revolve solely around me. Our success has been fueled by incredible people who embraced our vision, mission, and values, including my sons, Jarrin, Jennings, and Jentry. Even Joseph, my oldest son, and Kayla, while not actively involved in the business, have been supportive and encouraging on our journey. And of course, Kathryn could have squashed it very easily in the beginning, but she didn't, and her support was vital.

In business and life, you don't need all the details worked out beforehand to be successful. What you do need is a vision and conviction to live by time-tested principles centered around character. True character is not about climbing a mountain, standing on a summit, and shouting to the world, "Look at me, I did it! Have I told you lately what a great businessperson I am?" It is about the struggle, the failure, the fear, the self-doubt, and then, over time, learning enduring principles of truth that you can live by and find other incredibly capable people with similar values to join you on the journey.

The business of character is "walking by faith and not sight." It is not having the answers, not feeling capable of accomplishing the task at hand, but having a passion and desire to move forward, believing that if you remain true to core values, you can be satisfied with whatever happens in the end. For me, the business of character is about seeing how God has unveiled the way work can be so central to the mission of serving Him, how other people contribute and inspire in ways you could never predict, and how this thing called a corporation can be used to spin off blessings in countless ways. Employees, customers, the community, and investors can all benefit from the business of character.

For my part, I am determined to stay in the business of character.

—Jonathan Cotten, 2024

1

The Early Years: The Foundation of a Culture of Character

Let all that you do be done with love.
—*1 Corinthians 16:14 (NKJV)*

C haracter is integral to both your professional and personal lives. On the professional side, I now owned a business that would have character, and I was responsible for that. We named our company Easy Step Enterprises, LLC. We had a vision of wanting to help others take easy steps, but the steps up to that point had been anything but easy.

On the personal side, my character was being tested and developed each day. Earlier in life, I never dreamed that I would spend day after day by my daughter's bed, watching her endure unbelievable suffering. During one period in 2012, when she was hospitalized, she vomited every 15 minutes for 30 hours. Excruciating times like that will either make you or break you, and for me, it caused a complete reevaluation of my faith as a Christian and my purpose in life. In Psalms, we read: "God is our refuge and strength, an ever-present help in trouble. Therefore we will not fear, though the earth gives way and the mountains fall into the heart of the sea" (Psalm 46:1-2). In many ways, it felt like the earth had given way and the mountains had fallen into the heart of the sea, yet my family had found that refuge and strength in God—and now, I was poised to make one of the most dramatic changes in my life.

Becoming an entrepreneur was an integration of desires: to be home and present in my community rather than traveling so much, to have the freedom to apply lessons I had learned from working for great companies, and most of all, to launch out to bring even more purpose into my work than I previously had. As a national chain started in 1992, The Good Feet Store offered its franchisees a lot of freedom; I would have the privilege of setting the tone for my company, establishing its vision, mission, and values, and building my own brand in my own way.

I knew there were many other people out there like me who had been hurting. Some were runners like me; others were just people trying to live without pain. As the owner of this store, I could help them in non-invasive, non-pharmaceutical, and non-surgical ways to get the relief they needed. I could set my employee and customer experience standards and accept nothing less than the absolute best. I truly wanted our store to be a place where we transformed lives.

My passion for caring was fueled by walking with my daughter Kayla on her health journey. Having a front-row seat to not only her suffering but the suffering of so many other people was, in so many ways, a motivating force. There are enough lessons and stories from Kayla's health journey to fill an entire book.

Kayla's battle with mitochondrial disease has led to more than 50 hospitalizations and 100 visits to the ER, and they continue to challenge her and my family. When her health took another severe downturn in March 2022, we all sat down to have a long talk about the future, and I will always remember what she said.

"I'm tired of feeling terrible so much of the time," Kayla told us. "I'm tired of fighting, and I never want to go to the hospital again." As she explained to us, she wanted to go on palliative care: to have a hospice nurse who could look after her, manage her medications, and keep her comfortable so she could have more quality time instead of the fruitless search for a cure in the white sanitized halls of the hospital. As the doctors had told us again and again, there was no cure for her rare disease.

As heartbroken as we were, Kathryn and I were humbled by Kayla's bravery and faith. As she told us, she was not afraid to die; Kayla knew that when she died, she would spend eternity in Jesus's arms. In the meantime, she would keep up her faith, be the best person she could be, and cherish our time together. After our talk that day, Kathryn and I followed Kayla's wishes.

Through my love for my daughter, I've learned many hard lessons. Without Kayla's health challenges, it is doubtful that I would have increased my running mileage again and been able to complete a full marathon. If I hadn't done that, I would not have returned to The Good Feet Store a year later—with Kayla waiting in the car, remember—and heard Mary's offer to buy the business. Without the intense desire to be present and available in my hometown to be closer to Kayla, I would have likely never taken the risk of leaving a career of over 25 years, which required extensive travel, just to see if we could make a living another way. In short, Kayla's life story and her character are inextricably intertwined with our company's history.

How could we succeed? How could we beat the odds of a 50 percent rate of small business failure within 5 years and a 70 percent failure rate within 10 years, according to the Bureau of Labor Statistics[1]? How could we do this with limited financial resources, no prior experience as an entrepreneur, and no experience in the industry?

People said I was crazy, and maybe I was. I had no prior experience owning a business. However, now I was the president, CEO, COO, CFO, CMO, lead salesperson, inventory manager, and even the janitor for my business, Easy Step Enterprises, a franchisee of The Good Feet Store. Despite the challenges, my family had given me the confidence that I could succeed—and even if others didn't understand, the decision meant more to me than I could fully explain. I was beginning to see that my journey through plantar fasciitis and taking care of Kayla while she was so ill were deeply connected. Together, they were becoming a catalyst that would propel me into the next chapter of my life.

What I found as I progressed along my journey was less of a discovery and more of a confirmation of what I had known all along. Character is not ancillary to business. Rather, it is foundational to the company. Every business has a character, whether or not it is intentionally created.

If you are a business owner, you are responsible for the company's character. Regardless of the number of locations, you are responsible for the experience your employees and customers will have. An entrepreneur takes on this element of risk in addition to the financial risks involved.

If you are a leader but not an owner, you can still have that "owner's mindset" and be responsible for the character of your store or location. Will your location accept the company's minimum standards or go above and beyond to encourage customers to choose your business over others in the area?

Whatever level of employee or owner you are, you have the ability to impact the culture of the business. Character impacts every aspect of the business: values, employee relationships, metrics, customer service, and your network at large. Failure to focus on character is a failure to acknowledge the one thing that can impact the bottom line more than anything else.

If you have an A+ team in a store, they can compensate for slow traffic or a C location. If you have a C team in a store, the traffic could be significant, the store could be beautiful, and customer opportunities will still be lost. Many companies mistakenly dump money into marketing and beautiful locations without having an appropriate focus on character. When this is the process, money will always be left on the table. Prioritize character, and you will be able to see a difference. Your employees will be able to see a difference. Your customers will be able to see a difference. When you make it your business to focus on character, character will become your business. Before I became a business owner, I believed in this concept, but its value has been impressed upon me throughout my journey.

A defining trait of a business with character is a very specific mission. I knew, from our first day in business, that we were on a mission, but I had not clearly defined that mission. First, I had to understand the business I had purchased. What ingredients would make it a success? What unique offerings would set it apart from other companies? Why would customers support us, and what barriers might exist that we would need to overcome?

To answer these questions, I had to become intimately acquainted with our customers and our sales and service delivery process and understand the perspective of the people working in this environment every day. Caring would need to evidence itself by getting to the ground level, and in our case, sitting on a fitting stool, helping customers remove their shoes, and fitting them with arch supports.

This environment was quite a departure from dressing up in a suit, catching a plane to New York or Boston, and going into a conference room to make presentations to corporate customers. At times, it felt like a career regression, but then I would simply reflect that I was on a mission. Any misgivings would quickly evaporate, and I would press on. My new business was making a difference in people's lives. It was a joy to help a nurse, a carpenter, or an aspiring athlete get out of pain and become more active. Each success story increased my confidence in knowing that the arch supports had helped me and they could help thousands of other people.

The early years of a business are primarily about survival. You have to beat the extraordinarily high failure rate of small businesses. Surviving is about making your case in the marketplace, or as Dan Sullivan with Strategic Coach® says, "Test your ideas on people who write checks." An idea may seem cool, and you may even be passionate about it, but it has to appeal to enough people to be viable, and you have to deliver it efficiently enough to scale, even if your growth plans are modest.

In this crucible, a distinct and overarching business principle is driven home: Culture is meaningless unless it drives financial viability. Every employee should want their employer to be profitable. Every customer should want their store of choice to be profitable. Every community should want the companies that serve them to be profitable. Those principles should be axiomatic and obvious, but profit and business culture are sometimes seen as competitors, and nothing could be further from the truth.

We survived those first few years and learned a lot. In the early years, we desperately needed sales to maintain positive cash flow. Yet, it was not about just making a sale; there had to be integrity in what we were doing, and we would express that integrity in the care for employees, care for customers, and care for the impact on our community. Today, years later, at Easy Step Enterprises, the essence of what we do in our stores is to care for our customers. In almost every positive customer review we receive, there is at least some reflection on the care they received from our team members.

Seeing how so many people have cared for Kayla over the years has inspired me to take this commitment to care into our business. Proverbs 19:22 says, "What is desired in a man is kindness" (NKJV). Men and women, rich and poor, young and old, are all bound by this inextricable common denominator—the soul's response to kindness. In my mind, there is no higher aim for business owners than to have a company culture defined by excellence combined with sincere consideration for people, whoever they may be. To facilitate that culture, we need kindness, consideration, discipline, and integrity.

When we don't have experience in business, we often put the cart before the horse. We get hung up on all the processes, details, and specifics that we don't yet know, thinking those are the things that will make or break our success. In reality, processes and specifics can be trained, and they are relatively easy compared to the real work of business. Character, as expressed in traits like kindness, is difficult to teach and impossible to rush. It must develop over time, showing up in our personal lives before we bring it into our business.

This foundation of good character is not something businesses can ignore because culture emerges from it. It is always the result of many people of character working together. As such, culture needs to be taken seriously and cannot be left at the periphery of a business. It requires regular check-ins and adjustments. No business owner would go even a week without checking their bank account balances, and they certainly wouldn't go as long as a month or a quarter. Unfortunately, business leaders often go much longer than that without giving their culture any serious consideration.

When it comes down to it, everything in a business comes out of the culture. Culture directly connects to every meaningful metric that drives a company's success. It is the foundation of everything we do, and as such, business owners need a system to guide and nourish it.

Having said all this, the logical, million-dollar question that follows is:

How do you create a vibrant culture centered on character?

For starters, you need to know your "why." It can take some time to truly discover the "why" of your business. For some people, this can be very clear before their first day in business, and it seems that would be preferable. But for others like us, it might take working in the industry a bit, understanding the value proposition, and then establishing the cultural framework. Prematurely trying to establish these could create a faulty structure; however, defining the vision, mission, and values with confidence and clarity can lead to a more intuitive and natural process.

Each is distinct, though the symbiotic relationship between the vision, mission, and values should be pretty apparent. The combination of these things should connect to your life mission. For me to truly be inspired, I must fill the time from now until I get to heaven with meaningful work. Doing so takes the business of character beyond the realm of profit and loss statements and balance sheets into significance and great purpose.

When many of us think about culture, what comes to mind is only the mushy, feel-good stuff. Far too often, people write grandiose mission statements, jot down some values, put them on the wall, and then completely walk away. It's an easy mistake to make because the day-to-day challenges of running a business are often distracting and can pull us off course.

Developing a good culture in our businesses is a simple (but not easy) process. It involves defining the

Vision: What are the organization's directional headings, the GPS settings, or the north star?

Mission: What is the purpose or the fuel in the tank for the company?

Values: What principles will guide decisions and provide the flange on the wheel to keep everyone on track?

Taken together, the definitions, systems, and processes that come out of these elements work together to outline the culture of a business. That means that when done correctly, defining a company's vision, mission, and values isn't an academic exercise. As the DNA and the lifeblood of a business, they need to light a fire in you and your employees. They need to drive real *action*—the energy that motivates a person to test their character. That energy is contagious to a team of people sharing a similar perspective. It's how truly vibrant cultures can start to flourish. Properly constructed Vision, Mission, and Values challenge arrogance and instead foster humility. They are ideals that center us, confront us as needed, and point us on a solid path at every stage of growth and accomplishment. Michael Gerber, in his landmark book *The E-Myth Revisited*, speaks of "becoming what we are not without losing who we are." The Vision, Mission, and Values are the framework to make this happen.

"Culture eats strategy for breakfast" is a quote from legendary management consultant and writer Peter Drucker. A robust and healthy culture *is* a business strategy because it is the core driver of everything else an organization does. Such a culture is the beating heart of every successful business, and having one is the *only* way to achieve the kind of growth and success that is truly sustainable. Because of this, Vision, Mission, and Values are truly foundational, and defining all three takes patience and focus to get right. Let's take a closer look at Vision.

2

Vision: The GPS for a Company

Good leaders build products. Great leaders build cultures.
Good leaders deliver results. Great leaders develop
people. Good leaders have vision. Great leaders have
values. Good leaders are role models at work. Great
leaders are role models in life.
—*Adam Grant, The Wharton School professor and author*

The Vision of Easy Step Enterprises

Vision is not a destination that you ever reach. It is an
ideal that constantly reminds, refocuses, and recalibrates
everyone in the organization. Our vision at Easy Step
Enterprises goes beyond our products and services. It speaks
more to the role we want to play in people's lives, namely
our employees, customers, and community members. When

you put it all together, you get the "why" behind what we do, which is deeply rooted in the hearts and minds of our team members. The business model of The Good Feet Store is deeply relational, from employer to employee, to customer, and to the community. Our Vision statement is an effort to capture the potential of transformation in all these relationships. With all this said, the vision of Easy Step Enterprises is three-fold:

> **Vision: As an employer**, Easy Step Enterprises is focused on the well-being of our employees by providing a safe, respectful environment full of opportunity for anyone willing to embrace our Mission and Values. **As a retail business**, we sell more than solutions and comfort; our customers are buying hope. **As members of our community**, we walk beside people on their journey, regardless of their needs, because we are people who love our neighbors. We believe it is always more blessed to give than to receive.

My thinking about how we would relate to our employees was significantly shaped from the earliest moments of my career while at the lowest levels of the work hierarchy. After the ninth grade, I left public school. I didn't really feel like I fit in, and given my love for the outdoors and animals, I wanted to work on a farm. For some reason, my dad agreed, and I got a job making $3.25 an hour working at Oakencroft Farm, a beef cattle farm located outside of Charlottesville, Virginia. At night, I would do my schoolwork from home through a self-study correspondence course.

The value of understanding what a tough day at work is like created the context for how I thought about work on a fundamental level. For sheer physical exertion and a test of endurance, nothing for me has ever equaled picking up hay bales out of the field on an intense June or July Virginia summer day for 10-12 hours. The combination of the heat, throwing 60-pound hay bales around, and the dust from the hay leaves you so tired that you are not even hungry at the end of the day. That says a lot for a 16-year-old.

Not only does this define, in very personal terms, what working hard means, but it can also build appreciation for those who do intense physical work or have to labor under adverse circumstances.

If one of my primary goals of going into business were to engage in it as a mission to demonstrate by actions what an authentic Christian faith should look like, then caring for employees would be a primary test. Care and respect for those who worked hard and were on the front lines of the business was a priority then, and I pray they will always be a priority. Two verses from Proverbs illustrate this principle: "Do not withhold good from those to whom it is due, when it is in your power to act" (3:27) and "All hard work brings a profit, but mere talk leads only to poverty" (14:23). The first verse speaks to the employer's obligation not to take advantage of the least powerful in a corporate hierarchy. The second verse speaks to the incredible value added to an organization when employees work hard. It is a simple concept— respectful relationships will be fostered, while adverse and disrespectful relationships will erode.

George Washington Carver said, "When you do the common things of life in an uncommon way, you will command the attention of the world." Some people transform the work of everyday tasks into an art form through integrity, discipline, and mastery. I have never seen a business truly thrive without the presence of these heroes. They deserve good pay and good working conditions; a business culture should reflect this ethos. Although I never developed a mastery of manual labor, the early life experience of strenuous exertion at minimum wage influenced the Vision as it relates to employees.

Easy Step's Vision as an Employer

> *As an employer, Easy Step Enterprises is focused on the well-being of our employees by providing a safe, respectful environment full of opportunity for anyone willing to embrace our Mission and Values.*

After buying The Good Feet Store and thinking about the kind of company we wanted to build, the first consideration was to focus on employees rather than starting with customers first. A lot of the thinking behind it was influenced by Bill Fromm's book *The 10 Commandments of Business and How to Break Them*, specifically the first commandment. In his book, the first commandment to break is "The customer is king," which can cause a business to skip over the foundational aspect of caring for employees.

Sometimes, in business, employees can be made to feel as though they are powerless when engaging with customers. If a customer wants to berate or disrespect them, the employee can feel they are supposed to acquiesce. There is a joke that has stuck with me over the years that applies here. The story goes that an angry airline passenger was at the ticket counter venting his fury at the ticket agent. As he unleashed a tirade against this very polite young woman, the next passenger in line was amazed that she was totally unfazed. It was as if none of the angry travelers' insults or efforts at intimidation bothered her at all. Finally, she finished checking the man's bags and processing his ticket, and the next customer stepped to the counter. "How in the world do you handle that type of rudeness without it bothering you?" the man asked. "Oh, that's easy," the young ticket agent responded with a smile. "He is going to Miami and his bags are going to Seattle." Be careful, customers—it may be prudent not to act like a king.

Early on, as an owner, a university professor came into our store. From the start, he was challenging and adversarial with the arch support specialist. I could tell this was a fairly typical interaction for him and that he was no stranger to using forceful words and gestures to get the upper hand with others. Our employee took her job seriously and was passionate about what we did, and the customer's condescending attitude was bothering her. I called her aside and suggested I step in, which she eagerly accepted. I was not harsh with this customer, but I simply clarified that if we were to continue, mutual respect would be the framework. He ended up making a purchase and happily leaving with his arch supports.

There are times when employees need to press on with difficult customers, yet when the interaction crosses lines of respect, the employee should be protected. Knowing that company leaders have their backs at difficult moments gives employees confidence. It empowers them and actually makes them more effective with customer service. Customers respect empowered employees versus subservient ones.

There's nuance to applying this concept, but at Easy Step, we make it simple: we care for our employees so they can care for our customers. If you simply embrace "The customer is king" without thinking it through, you won't get the desired results. Ensuring customers are taken care of doesn't mean supplicating and saying whatever it takes to avoid uncomfortable moments. It involves listening and caring—but on another level, it involves authenticity.

Saying nice things to customers on the showroom floor of a business is good. Still, it's not very useful if, behind the scenes, business leaders are in any way creating conditions that foster disrespect for a customer. If the true mission of a business is to treat customers like "royalty," they must be treated that way by *everyone*, everywhere, and in all parts of the business. If customers are only treated well to their faces and the behind-the-scenes execution is chaotic and resentful, then all those polite words are only lip service.

It's a bit of a paradox, but this is what it means to "break" the first commandment Fromm mentions as a way to make it better. In a sense, for the customer to be treated like royalty, the *employees* must first be treated like kings and queens.

When defining a vision, businesses should remember that the employee and customer experiences are deeply connected. When people feel both safe and respected, they *relax*—and only then can you get an accurate picture of what strengths and weaknesses they bring to the table. Once you know that, you can deploy them the right way to pursue opportunities for themselves, the company, and the customers. Not doing this is where you get a disconnect between the goals of the company and those of its employees. A vision statement can sometimes put the focus on one or the other, but it is wise to have systems to account for both. As it relates to employees, business leaders can do this by providing a safe, respectful environment full of opportunity—but each part of that equation deserves a little more explanation.

Safe: "Safe" doesn't just mean physical safety or providing a workplace where people won't get injured. Safe means safe in *every* way, including mentally, emotionally, and spiritually. Having a place where people can come without being guarded about who they are is part of what leads to truly outstanding results.

It's important to tailor this to your employees' needs, as women and men often require different things to feel truly safe. As one example, Easy Step offers a flexible work environment for mothers with childcare responsibilities. Though we extend the same courtesy to working fathers, we wanted to create special allowances for mothers since they often bear most of the childcare responsibilities and often wrestle with career roadblocks because of the juggling required to meet their responsibilities.

Amanda joined us in the early days as one of the first five employees we hired after she responded to a Craigslist ad for an arch support specialist.[†] Her résumé was flawless, with no typos or grammatical errors, and all experience listed was relevant. It is interesting how, even today, a résumé that meets this basic threshold sets itself apart from so many others!

Amanda's work experience was primarily as a server at Texas Roadhouse for three years, which I found compelling; it was indicative of someone who didn't mind hard work and knew how to take care of customers. Amanda came on board and went through the basic on-the-job training we had at the time. Soon, she was helping customers, but she was painfully shy and would turn red when asked questions.

One day, she gave a customer a demo, and I passed her as she came through the door, bringing products back to the stockroom. I saw fire in her eyes. She was angry she hadn't made a sale, which communicated volumes to me. Desire is something you cannot teach, and to be successful in sales, business, or life, it's a baseline requirement, so working with her more, we tried to give her more and more opportunities.

Amanda went on to advance and lead in sales, moving to assistant manager, store manager, and then area sales manager. Then, in the summer of 2020, Amanda told us she had some news to share: she was pregnant and was very happy about it, although she planned to keep working. In time, however, it was apparent that this structure would not be compatible with her goals of being a mother, and she resigned.

[†] Yes, we used Craigslist as our talent recruitment strategy since we needed an affordable way to get our employment ads out there—not recommended as a cost-savings strategy, though it did lead us to finding Amanda, who is a diamond.

Employee departures are an inevitable part of business, but this one bothered me so much that I was not sleeping well at night. After a few days, I contacted Amanda and said, "This makes no sense. We are losing a valuable employee with an incredible knowledge base, and you are hitting reset on your career. At some point, you will need to start all over." Unfortunately, this is the story for many working mothers due to a lack of work accommodations. As leaders, we can do better than that in this technological age. We should not sacrifice childcare at the altar of career advancement.

Within a few weeks, Amanda rejoined us as a training manager, taking many of our sales processes, editing, organizing, and formatting them into executable training programs. One of the issues the pandemic revealed was that we had too much variance on a store-to-store basis, and variance is the enemy of scalability in business. We addressed this by having all new employees go through a formal training program in Richmond on their first week, an effort Amanda led by leveraging her sales demonstration capabilities in a highly consistent manner. We began to see better sales performance in our stores, as our teams now had a clearer sales structure in which to operate, made possible by creating a flexible environment where a working mother could thrive.

Respect: Similarly, a "respectful" environment says, "Regardless of where you come from or who you are—whether related to race, gender, abilities, and beliefs—you deserve basic respect as a human being." It's not particularly complicated, but it's amazing how many businesses still get it wrong.

While emotions can sometimes run high, a workplace should never devolve into degrading or condemning communication that pierces people's space and safety. Each person's integrity and respect should be inviolate, and even hard conversations should be accomplished constructively. Even when a business needs to use corrective action or terminate an employee, they should remember that both can and should be done with respect.

To do all this means understanding what your employees are going through and meeting their emotions with respect and understanding. One example occurred on a trip I took to our Lynchburg store, which was supposed to be routine. As I walked into the stockroom, I saw our employee, Jon, standing as if he were in a trance and not moving much when I came in.

"Is everything okay?" I asked, thinking he was just distracted or daydreaming. "I just found out that my father died," he replied. It took a second for what he'd said to register. *Did he just say his father died?* I had heard him correctly. Jon went on to explain that his father had been battling brain cancer, finally succumbing to it at the young age of 45. When he finished, I could only say one thing: "You need to go home, Jon." Only when I left the store did the enormity of what had occurred fully hit me.

Jon was an employee who had only been with us for three months and was now facing one of the biggest challenges of life: the premature death of a parent. He was only 21, and it was hard to imagine what he must have been facing. I found out about the arrangements for the memorial service and decided to drive down to Fayetteville, North Carolina, to the funeral home with my friend Benjamin Harris. The service progressed as expected until it came time for the eulogy when Jon got up to speak—as a 21-year-old—for his 45-year-old father.

What I witnessed was one of the most eloquent deliveries of any kind that I had ever heard. Jon was fully connected to the tragedy as he shared his experience. Still, as only a natural leader can do, he moved his focus to the audience, going beyond simple emotion and centering on eternal truths. With a clear and erudite grasp of Biblical truth, he shared the gospel of Jesus and how we can all be assured of entering heaven if we know Jesus as our Savior and Lord.

I left impressed that Jon had a deep sense of who he was with anchors for life. He had the capacity to feel the inevitable hurts of life while still processing them and leading others in such a healthy way with a strong sense of purpose that infused meaning into his life. It affected the way I viewed him at work as well, underlining the importance of respect and genuine connection between business leaders and their employees.

Caring for employees transcends mere obligations; it mirrors the compassionate role of a pastor nurturing their congregation. This profound responsibility extends beyond convenience or accolades. It is a journey of immersive learning, where employers gain valuable insights into the intricate tapestry of human experiences.

Since the day of his father's funeral, Jon has progressed through multiple advancements at our company, now having district manager responsibilities that reflect his character, abilities, and willingness to accept development feedback—which speak to the value of respect.

Opportunity: Providing a safe, respectful environment is essential, but there's still more to do to ensure employees perform their best. After all, if they feel like they are just pawns in a company's plan, why would they want to give their all to it? Without a chance to have any "skin in the game," where is the incentive to go above and beyond? When situations offer us no *opportunities* to grow, our instinct is to either check out or leave. At Easy Step, this is one of our deeper concerns when we talk about creating opportunity—because without doing so, all kinds of things begin to break down.

When a company stops pursuing growth for all, it ends up with growth's opposite: atrophy. The leadership gets comfortable and starts to coast, and the employees become disengaged and unaligned. Opportunities gradually disappear more and more. Soon, quality gets worse, and the competition closes in. These are all-too-common examples of how atrophy is a self-fulfilling cycle, reducing short and long-term opportunities more and more in a vicious downward spiral. For all these reasons, opportunity should be available to anyone and everyone whose character aligns with the company's goals.

Some front-line staff may be content to do the same jobs indefinitely, while others might want to grow their skills in new ways. Regardless of the details, each person in an organization should still be given chances to develop, grow, and be rewarded for their efforts. Growth should *not* be reserved as an exclusive perk for executives trying to climb the corporate ladder.

One concrete example of this at work is Laura Worosher, my executive assistant who joined us in February 2020. I met Laura on the sidewalk in front of the church one Sunday morning and was impressed with her family; the poise and charisma of then-five-year-old Tristan were particularly impressive, as he looked me in the eye and greeted me as if he were a politician running for office.

Through our connection at church, I learned that Laura previously managed a retail store. Now, she was homeschooling three children with enthusiasm and energy. Having observed Kathryn homeschooling our kids and having stepped in to carry that load myself at times, I knew this required great capability. If Laura could do this job with enthusiasm and excellence, she might be interested in part-time work as my executive assistant.

In January 2020, I contacted Laura to see if she would be open to working two days a week in the office. She said two days would be too much, but one day a week could work if I was open to it. I agreed.

Things were going smoothly until COVID hit, and on March 16, we shut down all 10 of our stores. After reviewing our costs, I realized that an executive assistant was a luxury I couldn't afford. The call to Laura the day we shut down was painful. "I am so sorry to have to do this, but we just can't afford your position," I said. "You have been such a help, but we are in survival mode." Graciousness is an ever-present attitude of Laura's, and this was no exception. Unfortunately, her graciousness just made me feel worse, and I hung up feeling like I had been gut-punched.

The next day, Laura called me. "I thought about this overnight and want to work for free. I love being a part of the company, and I want to help." Hearing her words, I think I cried. I thanked her but told her that wasn't an option, but we would figure something out. Over the first stages of the pandemic, her pay was meager, but it adjusted over time and worked out for both of us.

Over the years, Laura has brought talent and commitment that far exceeds the usual responsibilities of an executive assistant. She has been the primary planner of our Annual Team Meeting and other events with exceptional backstage organizational abilities and has even been onstage as an emcee. To be effective at facilitating, anticipating, coordinating, and advising on business matters requires strong intellectual capabilities and incredible emotional strength. She is as unoffendable as virtually anyone I have known in business, and she has been an incredible homeschooling mom, which is one of the most challenging jobs on the planet, requiring extraordinary capability. We will flex to accommodate an unusual work schedule to have access to the level of talent someone like Laura brings.

Easy Step's Vision as a Retail Business

The character of a business is often measured by the trust the customers have with the brand. A way to measure this is to look at the results of the interactions with those contacting the company the most (i.e., their best customers). Are their lives significantly enriched? Are they the most passionate advocates for the brand? Do they fare better after being patrons of the business or worse? The logical answer would be that the people spending the most money are the most passionate or feel the most positive about a given brand, but consider the case of Blockbuster Video in 2000.

An article from NBC News titled "Hubris-and late fees-doomed Blockbuster" explained more about reasons why Blockbuster's policies might have led to its downfall: "In 2000, Blockbuster collected nearly $800 million in late fees, accounting for 16 percent of its revenue."[2] The company collected these late fees because it was good for their financial statements, but it made many of their customers very angry, including some of their most loyal customers. This specific example comes from a company that is no longer in business, but there are many other examples of companies "selling their souls," to one degree or another, to make money, and who still do it year after year.

From the start, we believed that we could have a transformative impact on the lives of our customers, and we incorporated that belief into our Vision statement. We see this play out daily in our stores:

> *As a retail business*, *we sell more than solutions and comfort; our customers are buying hope.*

Being in a transactional business never appealed to me; I was not trying something that would only involve exchanging a commodity or setting up an efficient business model to generate a profitable income stream. What I *really* wanted, and why I was willing to take on so much risk by becoming a franchisee for The Good Feet Store, was a chance to make a difference in people's lives.

Having a business in the space of personal well-being makes the work so rewarding and motivating. Early on, when I worked every day in the store, it was amazing to see the effects on people struggling with issues that limited their ability to be active. People who were too tired and sore after a day of work to spend time with their friends. People who were in too much pain to walk their dogs or play with their children.

Too often, when we begin struggling with pain, we seek solutions that react to symptoms rather than address the cause of the pain, primarily because these solutions do not require a large commitment of time or money. They seem easy and straightforward, and that is what people gravitate towards. Many pharmaceutical models are built this way, and soon, customers are struggling with side effects that may be worse than the original problem.

To help people holistically pursue wellness, getting them active again and enjoying life, was inspiring. Some of this was connected to my personal experience, as I enjoyed becoming even more active in my 50s than I was in my 30s. It is exhilarating to run or pursue some other activity with my grandchildren or simply to retain fitness and good health as an example to them. I view health as a gift from God that I should steward with intention, and encouraging others to think the same way is a blessing.

Even as the wealthiest country in the world, America is often unable to provide care in an efficient and accessible way to many people. As I have stated, I have many healthcare heroes due to their care for Kayla and other family members, so this is not a broad criticism of healthcare workers. Yet, the system is often too bureaucratic, expensive, and impersonal. At The Good Feet Store, we seek to be the opposite. We have customers who come to us daily who have been almost drained of hope, and it is a joy to provide holistic solutions to their problems. The range of success stories extends from a pre-teenage boy in our Richmond store who found relief from significant heel pain to a 100-year-old woman in Rockville, Maryland, who left the store without her walker and told her daughter to "put that thing in the trunk." What a great business to be in!

Many people come to us with foot, knee, hip, or back pain, expecting to find a shoe store or a grab-and-go product. When they engage with our caring team members and find that Good Feet arch supports don't merely react to or mask symptoms but address the cause of the issue, they become raving fans. When people say, "I can't think of a better purchase that I've ever made," or "I've been dealing with my pain for years, and coming to your store changed my life," we are reminded of why we do what we do. Over the years, I've heard thousands of people say things like:

> "When I visited the store, I had pain in my heels and the balls of my feet. I immediately felt the results in my walking and posture."
>
> —Ann Mitchell, Easy Step customer

> "I tried all these products, and nothing worked. Finally, this took my pain away."
>
> —Teresa Perkins, Easy Step customer

> "If I had gotten these arch supports sooner, I could have two Super Bowl rings."
>
> —Michael Robinson, member of the
> Seattle Seahawks 2014 Super Bowl Team

> "My back doesn't hurt now as I walk down the 18th fairway."
>
> —Amanda Sambach,
> University of Virginia championship golfer

Hearing these types of testimonials is truly a joy. Being involved in a business where you can offer people hope and change their lives is deeply rewarding and powerful.

To be in the business of character, love for customers is an essential ingredient. Not love for their money but love and care for them as individuals with a desire to help them, whether they can purchase anything or not. When customers come into one of our stores and cannot pay for arch supports or qualify for any of our financing options, they think they've arrived at the end of the road. Seeing their surprise and joy when we can extend to them our Good Feet/Good Hearts program and fit them with our 3-Step System of arch supports at no cost has had a transformational effect on our customers and our employees. We use a social media platform where employees frequently share their stories. What an incredible inspiration to our people to see that our work is not only about meeting a financial goal. Instead, our vision is about uplifting others and addressing the needs of marginalized people specifically.

Easy Step's Vision as a Community Member

Finally, the third part of our vision statement brings everything together:

> *As members of our community, we walk beside people on their journey, regardless of their need, because we are people who love our neighbors. We believe it is more blessed to give than to receive.*

The phrase "giving back" is often used when a company supports charitable causes in the community. Others have made the point, and I agree, that this phrase can sound like a successful company is taking something inappropriately from the community and then has to "give back." If a company is truly in "the business of character," the contributions to the community should be evidenced in manifold ways. Great jobs are created for workers, customers are served with integrity, and other businesses are supported as supplier partners. Every employee, every customer, and all the members of the community have a vested interest in wanting companies to be profitable and growing. When we think of the last part of our Vision statement, it is not an apology for being successful. Rather, it is an opportunity to use the power of a business to make an external impact and to provide one of the most powerful sources of inspiration for all of us internally.

Inspiring people to love is a great mission. At Easy Step, it is beneficial to repeatedly remind ourselves of the benefits of loving others and walking with them on their journey regardless of their needs. We have countless examples of people we've been able to help, and sometimes without receiving any financial reward.

One powerful thing that businesses can do is be incredibly agile in addressing the community's needs by working with local nonprofits. At Easy Step, we've implemented our Community Partner Program for this purpose, which makes careful determinations about which potential nonprofit partners are fiscally well-managed and have missions aligned with ours so our contributions can have a measurable impact. Our criteria make it so that we usually end up working with many smaller nonprofits, but each one is always financially responsible, allowing us to realize our intended results.

In addition to helping these incredible nonprofits, when our employees can get involved with these community partners, they find motivation and purpose challenging to measure. Human beings crave purpose, and dissatisfaction at work is often connected to a lack of purpose. It is difficult to describe the impact of things like:

- Engaging with someone in a prison jumpsuit who is working to establish a future after incarceration

- Helping someone who has lived their entire life in public housing but is now pursuing a dream of owning their own home one day
- Sharing tears with a TAPS family member as they recount their memories of a fallen military loved one

These are not imaginary examples but a sample of hundreds of interactions we have experienced. Our relationship with our Community Partners is not due to feeling guilty about having a profitable, successful business but rather to seeing our business as a powerful resource that can be deployed to fuel the great work that others are doing to address the needs of our communities. A side benefit is that our team members often comment about it being one of the most motivating aspects of their jobs.

Vision and Culture

Culture is an oft-discussed topic in business and organizational settings, and a toxic culture is often recognized as a cause of business failure. Yet, at times, an emphasis on positive culture can be dismissed as the "soft side" of business and disconnected from hard business drivers. Suppose you do not tie culture to a meaningful business structure. In that case, you will fail to arrest a toxic environment or, alternatively, become a meaningless accessory to a successful product or service business.

Early in my entrepreneurial journey, I wanted to establish a culture to drive actionable business results while leaving a positive wake as we touched employees, customers, and our community. The sequence of that progression was intentional: employees, customers, and community. Particularly in a retail or service business, how you treat employees becomes vital to sustainable success. All things being equal, profits will follow if your employees are happy and your customers are happy. It was that philosophy that informed our vision statement.

For emphasis, I will repeat that a vision statement is a company's north star or GPS, and when determining direction, it is used as an ideal rather than a "goal." A company never fully arrives at its vision because if it did, it would immediately start to atrophy due to complacency or arrogance. The goal is to make a vision statement lofty enough to capture and inspire the imagination while being realistic enough to help a company track its consistency with its ideals. Doing so begins to sketch both the desired outcome and the strategies to get there.

One last thing to keep in mind is that many people equate growth and success with "inevitable tradeoffs" that require a lack of care for people. I have resisted this idea and refuse to believe it. For everyone to feel both successful and personally fulfilled, a company's vision must run through its company from top to bottom rather than living only in the heads of a couple of its leaders.

It's why the vision must be shared among the employees, so each person is encouraged to grow, as it's the only way to make growth sustainable. Once a company loses its vision or "why," the sacrifices it must make to grow are no longer worth it, and the employees all get burned out. But if we wake up each day driven to help our coworkers, clients, and community, we will end up doing so in meaningful ways and will be able to bear the "how."

Defining Your Vision Statement: Questions for Reflection

Whether you are an employee or a business owner, to fulfill your life purpose, your work and life must be aligned, and your daily work needs to inspire you. In your life, this comes down to knowing your character—and in business, it means aligning everyone's personal growth with the organization's vision, mission, and values.

Setting aside compensation and benefits, what we do every day needs to feel significant. Our concern can't simply disappear when the day is over; we need to do meaningful work that has lasting consequences. All of this is the reason that our vision starts with our employees. We want them to prosper, not just reach certain milestones. If we don't get that right, it compromises everything else we do—but if we do get it right, the possibilities are endless.

Your vision will transform interactions with customers that would typically be transactional. A strong vision statement is the first step businesses must take to realize this dream. With all this in mind, here are some exercises and questions to think about as you put together your own comprehensive vision statement:

For internal stakeholders (primarily the employees):

1) What does their day-to-day experience look and feel like?
2) In simple terms, what will best express what employees want in their work environment?
3) How will employees know how to empower and develop themselves and others while maintaining high standards?

For customers:

1) How does engaging with your company affect a customer immediately after a sale? What about after consistent engagement with your company and the products and services you offer? Defining this will speak to your value proposition—and the greater the impact, the more powerful the business model.
2) If the internal policies and practices regarding customers were published on a physical or digital billboard, would you be confident or concerned?
3) If you were asked to provide a list of enthusiastic customer advocates for your brand, would that list have to be curated carefully, or could that list be readily compiled from customer interactions in the last month?

For the community at large:

1) *Does your company's presence create gratitude from the community for multiple reasons?*
2) *How will you ensure the company's influence—on employees, customers, the environment, and the most vulnerable—will be net positive? Will the company have to exploit one or more of those areas and compensate it for another?*
3) *My friend and colleague, Dan Silverman, likes to ask, "If we didn't exist any longer as a company in a community, would our absence be felt? In what way would this void be felt?"*

3

Mission: Fuel for the Journey

With a Vision to serve as a GPS or North Star by which to navigate, a company next needs a way to begin moving in that direction. Like preparing for a long journey, the next step is to fill the tank of the Enterprise with the fuel of purpose. This is the company's *mission*, the *raison d'être*, or the *why* of every process or organizational action.

To understand how Easy Step built its Mission statement to build on its Vision, we need to understand what a great Mission statement looks like—what it does when it's working and what happens when it isn't. These can vary quite a bit, but what's important overall is to make sure it *aligns with but is distinct from* your vision statement and that it *aligns with but is distinct from* your values.

To illustrate this a bit, consider a few of these mission statements from major companies in different industries:[3]

Chick-fil-A: "To be America's best quick-service restaurant at winning and keeping customers."

TED: "Spread ideas, foster community, and create impact."

Warby Parker: "To inspire and impact the world with vision, purpose, and style."

Chick-fil-A views its connection to customers as relational and extending past the immediate transaction. To be engaged in "winning and keeping customers" involves creating an experience that produces positive emotions that extend past the moment a meal is consumed. TED is an organization known for its inspirational talks, but again, they are not strictly an *event* company. According to their mission statement, they want to create community-level impact through the spread of ideas and will do it however makes sense for their business model. Finally, Warby Parker makes prescription glasses of all kinds—but the *way* they do it is what guides them (speaking to their values with a "vision" and "purpose" of ethical business practices, executed with "style").[4]

With these examples in mind, here's how Easy Step approached writing a mission statement of our own.

The Mission of Easy Step Enterprises

As a leading franchisee of The Good Feet Store, we sell arch supports. However, our mission is not to sell products. More accurately, our business is to help people either prevent pain or address the cause of their pain so they can enjoy the highest level of activity possible. After thinking this through a little more, our mission statement at Easy Step Enterprises became:

"Helping our community live an active and healthy lifestyle, one step at a time."

Like some examples in the previous chapter, we tried to align with our Vision (with distinct aims as an employer, a retail business, and a community member) and our Values, which we'll cover in the next chapter. The way we wrote it, our ultimate mission was not to "sell foot-related products" or "help people get out of pain," even if those are both things that we do daily. Instead, we set ourselves up to have a more expansive purpose that spoke to all the different aspects of our organization: having care for the well-being of our employees in all areas of their lives, being invested in helping customers pursue true holistic health, and engaging with community partners who are making an impact.

For me to feel I owned a successful business, it could not be one focused on simply selling customers a product; we needed to make a real difference in their lives. I knew firsthand how arch supports had transformed my life, and I knew they could do the same for others in so many ways. They could help people run again, work 12-hour shifts in the emergency room without foot pain, dance, walk their dogs, walk to the grocery store, avoid costly and painful surgery with long recovery periods, and more. In short, it was something that could help people without hope *get their lives back.* This has always been my mission, and it fills our workdays with purpose and inspiration.

Following is a Google review from Joyce about her experience in our Leesburg store:

Exceptional customer service from start to finish! The store manager went above and beyond the call of duty, ensuring every detail and concern was met. Again, Leadership in Action! Her entire team deserves recognition for all that they do each day.

Another Google review from LaDawn, a customer who visited our Newport News store, shared her satisfaction from a different perspective:

> I am brand new to life in Hampton Roads. I am a Midwest woman who absolutely adores all 4 seasons and is not afraid of snow or ice. I genuinely miss home. My time in Virginia up until now has been catastrophically inhumane. The entire experience of moving across the country due to the pandemic, displacing employment and entire life, was hard. To move with the hope of starting over while having employment here was a light, but still, we were homeless. Being homeless was by far one of the cruelest and most inhumane and undeserved experiences of my life. Then, having both my Yorkie sons die 7 months apart last year took grief to a new level, and my health plummeted. I have struggled to find professional, humane, knowledgeable, compassionate, and competent health care here too.
>
> So, during the last week of March, at the urging of my adult goddaughter, I went to see about inserts for my feet. Homelessness changes your ability to provide the care needed for your physical, emotional, mental, and spiritual health. I live with plantar fasciitis, bone spurs, and completely flat feet. I had not had proper shoes, inserts, compression socks, or sleeve support for my feet and ankles [for] 4 years. When I walked into the store, I was literally hunched over. I could not stand upright; I shuffled my feet one at a time, and every inch was as painful as if I was stepping on nails with hardened cement around my ankles.
>
> Upon entering the store, I was amazed. The store looked like a professional yet welcoming and comfortable medical facility. Each potential customer had their own private cubicle space as if it were a private doctor's office or a

cubicle at a financial institution. How wonderful that people could discuss the intimate needs of their foot health and all financial decisions with dignity. I met with Mr. Ben, who literally was my personal concierge [for] better foot health and better living. My maternal grandmother used to say, "When your feet hurt, your soul hurts." She was right. Mr. Ben did an extensive workup of my history and took measurements and a print of my feet. We discussed foot care at length in a manner no foot or ankle specialist had ever taken the time or care to spend with me about my own health.

After my consultation, Mr. Ben brought out both shoes and inserts that literally changed my life in seconds. He taught me which inserts to wear, and we took several walks around the store with the new shoes and inserts. Now, if you stayed with me this long, you know I came in bent down. After the consultation and inserts, I was walking upright. That may not mean much to you, but that was a miraculous moment for me. Mr. Ben and the entire store family restored not only my ability to stand upright and walk without pain. They restored my faith in humanity that day. I highly recommend you and anyone you love or care for to run, shuffle, or skip to The Good Feet Store. Very few things, especially business transactions, leave you feeling better about yourself, let alone life. But this one did for me. I hope, with all my heart, your visit does the same for you.

These are just two examples of many testimonials, the combined result of which is a mission realized. When these testimonials are shared throughout our company in our company calls, on our social media platform, or in other ways, it infuses our employees with inspiration and purpose. Most people want greater purpose and a conviction that they are making a difference in their work. Money as a primary motivator is insufficient.

The careful thought put into our mission statement has had all kinds of ripple effects. It becomes essential to take the words off the page and actually execute them in your business at all levels. To do so, all employees have to buy in and be aligned—which means hiring people with character at the beginning and then creating a workplace culture that encourages people to align with our mission.

In a sales-driven business, whether a retail business like ours or in a business-to-business environment, the confidence of the people selling is crucial. They are the first ones to be persuaded that the value proposition is good. If we feed everyone on the team a constant stream of customer success stories with testimonials saying, "This is the best purchase I ever made," "This changed my life," or "I got my life back," we create internal, intrinsic motivation. When the mission is authentic and powerful and is consistently validated by the customers, the business's fuel tank is refilled automatically. The result is employees who are more organically motivated.

Encouraging customer testimonials motivates the employees, who then turn more customers into raving fans who leave testimonials, creating a very positive flywheel. The truth is, it is easy to create a positive customer experience in our stores. When customers come to us, they are often disillusioned and can feel their hopes dimming. Many of the products and services in the footcare industry are inadequate to meet the customer's needs. Having a drive and passion for "helping our community live an active and healthy lifestyle" can be equivalent to offering water to a thirsty traveler, especially when we get the "helping" part right. Jesus said that offering a cup of cold water in his name would be significant (Mark 9:41), and once I saw a business as a mission outpost, it was very inspiring.

CarMax, the nation's largest used-car retailer, created an entire business model around an elegant solution to one of the most hated transactions by most people: engaging with a used car salesperson. As their website outlines:

> As the original disruptor of the automotive industry, our "no-haggle" prices transformed car buying and selling from a stressful, dreaded event into the honest, straightforward experience all people deserve.

Their recent celebration of 20 straight years on the Fortune 100 Best Companies to Work For list is indicative of a vibrant and healthy culture, with employees buying into their Mission.

The mission of a business is critical to ensure the whole culture is actionable and connected to meaningful business drivers. To address the criticism of a culture centered around Vision, Mission, and Values as mere words on a wall, the Mission needs to be carried out not simply in sales but in operations, customer service, and every department. When everyone in the company can participate in the success stories of the customers, it unifies everyone's efforts. Without this unifying aspect, it can be easy to make a sale but fail to provide the appropriate customer service follow-up, compromising the whole mission. Things such as training and creating operations process manuals take on new meaning and significance, as they are highly central to fulfilling the Mission.

To help think this through, consider some of the following exercises and questions as you sit down to write your mission:

Defining Your Mission Statement: Thoughts for Reflection

A mission statement will drill down on top of a vision statement, explaining more of what a business's operations will aim for and how it will accomplish its goals. For a company dedicated to leading with strong character, its mission statement should:

1) **Be specific enough to evoke an image of what the company is engaged in.** *Vague statements that could apply to a vast number of companies will be ineffective.*

2) **Capture the net positive effect it has on the best customers.** *Are the best customers' lives dramatically enhanced by the product or service? If so, you simply use creativity and the most concise description of the benefits to craft a mission statement.*

3) **Be rooted in reality and not promise something unachievable.** *A customer should find the mission statement to be credible.*

With their vision and mission statements handled, business leaders can get even more specific: they can outline their *values*, bringing everything together in day-to-day operations.

4

Values: The Guide Rails to Stay on Track

Even if it is not explicitly stated, every business has a values system that flows from and in accordance with the values of its leadership. As the founder of my fledgling business, I wanted to be intentional about establishing the right values, which required thought and reflection. The values had to align with *my* beliefs, but I had to make sure they were inclusive and allowed room for different perspectives— they couldn't discriminate against talented people who were aligned with my vision and mission but thought or believed differently than I did.

Circling back to the examples offered in the mission section, each of the companies mentioned has its own distinct values. Here's a quick look at what each one thought was most important to accomplishing its goals:

Chick-fil-A: "We're here to serve; We're better together; We're purpose-driven; We pursue what's next."[5]

TED: "Curiosity, reason, wonder, and the pursuit of knowledge—without an agenda."[6]

Warby Parker: "Innovation, integrity and impact."[7]

CarMax: "Do the right thing; Put people first; Win together; Go for greatness

Looking closely at these, we can start to see how many different ways to accomplish a mission and vision and what a huge impact those values will have on a company's culture. At Chick-fil-A, customer service is valued in such a way that the entire quick-serve industry emulates their "my pleasure" approach. This is accomplished through cohesive teamwork and focusing on a mission greater than just serving food. Finally, being forward-thinking has led to their evolution from being mall-based to serving customers walking into their restaurants to developing some of the most efficient drive-thru operations in the industry.

TED takes a different approach. They explicitly state they want to spread ideas "without an agenda" but do so following their core principles. These include "reason" and "the pursuit of knowledge" on the one hand, but also "curiosity" and "wonder" on the other; in other words, not all the ideas they share through the world need to be 100 percent *right* for all time, but they should always spark discussion and push things forward.

Warby Parker keeps things simplest of all: in their products, they will focus on "innovation" at all levels (from the designs themselves to the materials they use). In business decisions, they will use "integrity" to not compromise on the most important aspects of their mission and vision—and the end result of all the above will be "impact" that they can measure. CarMax, as the used car industry disruptor, focuses on its people and the integrity of the sales transaction since that was the historical pain point for customers in the used car industry.

The Four Values of Easy Step Enterprises

With some of this context in mind, Easy Step is still guided by the four values that we came up with initially—and they still challenge us today to live in a manner that both enhances our image and pushes us to continue to grow and develop, personally and professionally:

RADICAL INTEGRITY: Wholeness, alignment, consistency. It's the courage to truly see ourselves, relate to others, and face the demands of reality.

PASSIONATE PERSUASION: Believing to the core in the value of our products and services. We participate in transforming lives, achieving dreams, and realizing potential. We are unabashed advocates for the health and well-being of our customers.

UNWAVERING POSITIVITY: Expressing joy in being a problem-solver, a collaborator in wellness, a proponent of enjoying life. In a world weary with anxiety, we choose to be messengers of hope.

PERSISTENT DILIGENCE: Having a champion's commitment to excellence. We embrace the truth of the timeless proverb: "Slack habits and sloppy work are as bad as vandalism" (Proverbs 18:9, MSG).

With all this said, let's look at each one of these in a little more detail.

"Radical Integrity"

Wholeness, alignment, consistency. It's the courage to truly see ourselves, relate to others, and face the demands of reality.

Dr. Henry Cloud's book *Integrity* helped shape my thinking about this value, along with seeing this value implemented at my previous employer, Plus Relocation Services. We often think of integrity as something that starts with another human being. Yet, it has to start with an inward look first. In life and relationships, I've found that the hardest thing to do is to look in the mirror. As I engage with others who are committed to integrity, they share the same struggle. We tend to either flatter ourselves too much or depreciate our value and ability to contribute. Having the ability to take a fair and honest appraisal of ourselves is essential to healthy relationships and accomplishing our goals in a balanced way, and that is what Radical Integrity is all about.

Pastor Chuck Swindoll shared a great story about some children forming a club. They came up with these three rules:

1) Nobody act big.
2) Nobody act small.
3) Everybody act medium.[8]

That is a great guide for a children's club and also for a business. Acting "medium" is to have wholeness and the courage to truly see ourselves.

To help instill this value from the very beginning, I ask our new employees during their first week what comes to mind when they hear the word "integrity." The answers are often about being honest and accountable, which is good, but Radical Integrity goes beyond that. It is not primarily about my actions towards others but who I am at the core of my being.

When an individual embraces Radical Integrity, it becomes much easier to face the demands of reality. As an example, salespeople can sometimes struggle to face the demands of reality by not accepting the outside challenges that can make meeting a sales goal difficult. Business leaders might hear things like "Traffic was low today," "The economy is trending down," or "The weather is bad" as reasons for lower performance. Each of these things can be true, but someone who embraces Radical Integrity will face these challenges with courage—and the result is often either a strong performance despite obstacles or learning to set up future success. This mindset is crucial in sales and virtually every other area of business, and Radical Integrity is its foundation.

When we speak about Radical Integrity, we ask, "Is this an event or an ongoing process?" It obviously has to be a process; life changes, and to remain whole, we also have to change and adjust to life. This requires being self-aware, allowing others to speak the truths we need to hear, and turning off the noise and distractions so we can tune into what's happening inside us.

It is challenging to stay focused this way or be so introspective. Because of that, each of us must be settled in who we are as people—otherwise, we will be out of alignment in the workplace and when trying to establish effective working relationships. Another foundational verse from the Bible has transformed me and has a great impact on others: "For you created my inmost being; you knit me together in my mother's womb. I praise you because I am fearfully and wonderfully made; your works are wonderful, I know that full well" (Psalm 139:13-14). We are not a cosmic accident but an intentional creation by our loving heavenly Father. Embracing both our value and the uniqueness of who we are is essential to having Radical Integrity.

This value also comes into play when we hold our employees accountable for their metrics: when it comes to meeting goals, all of our employees must demonstrate Radical Integrity. After all, if we don't live up to this value, we are either devastated by or in denial about gaps we see in our performance. Our emphasis on Radical Integrity is centered on the concept that strength must be built from the inside out. We have to know who we are and *why* we are doing what we are doing before we can master the "how" and the "what" of our jobs.

On a personal note, for me as a Christian, the concept of grace allows me to truly embrace Radical Integrity. The truth of Romans 5:8 defines grace. "But God demonstrates His own love toward us, in that while we were still sinners, Christ died for us" (NKJV). The only way that I can look in the mirror and reconcile my failures is by embracing the grace of God. Knowing that I am forgiven and loved by God removes the burden of striving to achieve perfection. We are loved completely by our Creator, and nothing we do will either increase or diminish His love.

Systems to Reinforce Radical Integrity

As we seek to instill this and the other values in our teams, the various elements have to be unpacked so they understand the true depth of the principle.

Wholeness: At a high level, "wholeness" encompasses everything else about this value, including "alignment" and "consistency"—because if something is whole, it has all the necessary parts in place within itself. Wholeness requires self-reflection, and as leaders, carving out quiet time for reflection and introspection is critical. This is character calibration, which requires a plumb line or form of measurement to calibrate to. I pray that what I profess and what I possess, as far as motivation and goals, are aligned. Self-awareness is an ongoing process that requires introspection and the willingness to hear others' input. A leader is in a dangerous place if they develop an "echo chamber" of "yes" people with similar perspectives. There should be appropriate challenge and accountability, especially when a leader veers off course.

Alignment: This is a Day 1 emphasis with our new team members. Our current society often shies away from the concept of objective truth. We don't because we believe in old-fashioned truths like good and evil, right and wrong, you met the standard, or you didn't. The entire business model is based on this, regardless of how inconvenient the truth is. Try going to the bank and explaining that you wrote $25,000 more in checks than you have in the account. The bank will emphasize that it believes in objective truth. Either the money is there, or it is not.

Consistency: This is a simple concept, yet often we don't see consistency as a display of Radical Integrity. The airline industry measures on-time departures and arrivals as a significant metric because the trust of the customer is centered on it. Can I depend on you to get me from Chicago to Miami when you say you will? Reliability creates safety and security in all of our relationships. Instilling the value of simply this element of culture is critical to an organization's success.

The courage to truly see ourselves: In any relationship, especially when there is conflict, our natural inclination is to look at the other person involved and see their fault. Integrated character gives us the capacity to look in the mirror, see the warts and all, and go out into the world in peace. Another incredible book that was so foundational for me was *Boundaries* by Dr. Henry Cloud and John Townsend. Accurately seeing ourselves comes first, enabling us to see what we do or do not own in a relationship.

To relate to others: When we accurately see ourselves, we exponentially increase the odds of relating well to others. When we are aware of our own faults, we will not be as inclined to judge, assume, and condemn when we see the faults of others. When we can celebrate our success properly, we will naturally want to celebrate and encourage the success of others.

To face the demands of reality: Resiliency indicates someone who embraces Radical Integrity. People who face life's storms with courage and allow these "demands of reality" to build depth of character inspire me. Then, I encounter others whose entire day is thrown off because their coffee was not prepared properly in the drive-thru. The day may bring weather issues, bad economic news, a pandemic, traffic jams, or bad coffee, yet Radical Integrity provides us with the courage to face them all successfully.

Workplace Application: If leaders model this behavior first, it will be much easier to create an environment that gives the employees the courage to face reality. Some key elements to apply this are:

> *Allow failure.* A culture that sees failure as part of healthy development is able to discern mistakes that emanate from violating values and from mistakes that come from lacking capability or development. Instill respect for values while simultaneously removing the fear of making mistakes.

> *Create clarity around standards.* Structure creates security, and that structure should be communicated with as much detail as possible. It is highly unlikely that the

visionary entrepreneur will do this, so make sure there are vision-catchers on the team who have the ability to be detail-oriented and extend it into a process.

Coach and don't condemn. If there is regular account-ability in a coaching style, then high-character employees will seek it out. Condemning messages laced with shame will create fear-based, dysfunctional cultures.

"Passionate Persuasion"

Believing to the core in the value of our products and ser-vices. We participate in transforming lives, achieving dreams, and realizing potential. We are unabashed advocates for the health and well-being of our customers.

When I first wrote our values, I left this one out—but then I considered that we were a sales-driven business, and hello, we better address sales in our values, as it is the most basic business driver. But how do we do this so that it is con-sistent with other values? How can it be expressed so it has authenticity and can be public facing so a customer reading it would be reassured? It was also important that this value is not just for those directly involved in sales because every member of a team should believe in what the company does and the impact it has.

Because of this, Passionate Persuasion is a sequential value. First, each team member must believe in the products and services they provide to customers—if they don't believe in it, how in the world can they influence anyone to spend their hard-earned money on it? In our business, this looks like fitting each employee with a personalized system of arch supports on their very first day.

Our employees are encouraged to pay close attention to how they adjust to wearing the arch supports because developing a personal story about their experience with the product is critical. Each team member must understand the functionality of the products on an experiential level, not just a conceptual level. As they experience better alignment, improved balance, and the elimination of aches and pains, they will be more authentic as they connect with customers.

Second, as they participate in transforming lives, achieving dreams, and realizing potential, they are encouraged to *enter into* our customers' stories. They are not selling someone a product but rather walking alongside someone and going through a journey together. By doing this, they see what a product does for someone firsthand, and they have ownership over its impact, which helps make them unabashed advocates.

Finally, when it comes time to discuss the price, our employees can do so without blinking, hesitating, or being uncomfortable. When they do get objections, they don't grab a business card and a brochure; instead, they follow up with questions and continue sharing our story from a place of *true belief* in what we do. With all these things in place, employees build their confidence, and our value proposition becomes clear, fostering an unapologetic approach to making the actual offer.

The longer I am in business, the more I believe that sales is the area of a company that potentially requires the closest alignment to values. Part of the reason that sales can be detached from values and culture is the belief that it will impede meeting sales targets if there is too much focus on culture. Sometimes, people think that you can't be successful if you are not ruthless and refuse to stretch the truth. Successful selling should emanate from a core conviction of authenticity that leads the customer in a natural way to a successful close.

When hiring new team members, a sales background is not always positive, and sometimes, it can be a red flag. I received a piece of wisdom from my friend, author Wayne Jacobsen, which I've since adopted as a code of my own:

"Anytime my success in life depends on another person's response, I will manipulate them." There's a lot of truth to what Wayne says because manipulation is often the main umbrella under which sales methods are historically taught and trained. A primary reason that sales as a profession has such a stereotypically bad reputation is due to manipulation being used as a common tactic. But sales, in my view, should not be that way. Instead, at Easy Step, we teach our employees to embrace the value of Passionate Persuasion. We want them to understand what our products *do* and what impact they have on people's lives on a personal level.

Over time, as they stay attentive and engaged, they begin to see the constant flow of success stories from customers. As they become personally convinced through seeing our results, selling becomes a natural, organic, and intuitive process for them. To that point, we have no five-star reviews that say, "Your business card transformed my life. I got your brochure, and my life totally changed." Instead, our customers leave with our products and a great experience with our team, and their reviews reflect how it improved their lives. *That* is the way that we still value performance in sales while reframing what it means to "sell."

Systems to Reinforce Passionate Persuasion

Even though this value largely applies to how we approach sales, it is closely aligned with Radical Integrity and is designed to remove inordinate pressure from either the salesperson or the customer. It was these key aspects that helped us further define our systems and processes:

Genuine Sales Philosophy: Many sales approaches and tactics are flawed because they rely on and encourage the employees to sell customers a product or service they don't really need. Behind closed doors, the sales team is instructed to do things that are in the company's best interest at the customers' expense. A sales philosophy should rest first on convincing the sales team of the inherent value of the offering. Once the salesperson believes, the work of convincing the customer is well underway. A confident and caring salesperson creates trust with the customer by implementing this simple formula:

Congeniality + Competence + Trust = Sales Success

Congeniality is the ability to form a very positive first impression. A pleasant, confident demeanor consistent with our unique personality gets the relationship started with the customer on the right foot. Competence is being skilled and knowledgeable about our products and services. Trust is formed when congeniality and competence are combined into a safe, caring package where the customer can trust the guide. Sales success follows. Passionate Persuasion is designed to foster living out this formula.

Employee Experience: One of the first steps in our training process is to fit each new team member with our 3-Step System of Good Feet arch supports. By experiencing our products themselves, they typically end up truly believing in what we do and understanding the transformational value of the products we sell. When a new team member says, "I just want to help people," our response is, "Great! The best way to do that is to help them leave with Good Feet arch supports in our shopping bag because that is how we get raving reviews." Sales metrics then become a measuring stick as to how well the employee embraces the value of Passionate Persuasion. Have they embraced using the products themselves? Do they understand how it helps our customers? Do they understand the value proposition, especially as it relates to other products on the market? With affirmative answers to these questions, the issue of the team member's confidence is answered, and the sales performance will follow.

Customer Engagement: Finally, seeing the genuine belief and empathy that our salespeople bring to the sales floor, our customers don't feel manipulated or taken advantage of. Instead, they are engaged in the sales process, and if they buy our products, they do so willingly and in a positive state of mind. They have faith that we are working to improve their lives—which in turn makes them advocates for our products, for the culture of our company, and as members of their community.

"Unwavering Positivity"

Expressing joy in being a problem-solver, a collaborator in wellness, a proponent of enjoying life. In a world weary with anxiety, we choose to be messengers of hope.

Simply being a positive, "glass-half-full" person is not enough for business success. Often, to get a positive outcome, there must be an ability to accurately see a problem, the capacity to embrace it, and the ability to solve it. Many business models do not even pretend to solve problems, and some actually *create* problems for their best customers (the tobacco industry, for example, has been killing some of its best customers for centuries). Not everyone is in that same extreme category; some simply offer band-aids or distractions from customers' problems.

Still, a business that can consistently solve customers' problems has a leg up when it comes to creating a dynamic culture. For our part, we see a consistent hunger among our employees to be involved in work that has a great purpose. A key component of their training, then, is helping them have the capability and *capacity* to solve problems. Because overwhelmingly, the people that come into our stores have a problem. When they come in, we must be ready to engage with them: we need to have the mental and emotional capacity to focus on their problems.

There are times when problem-solving is not needed, but being a messenger of hope is. Sometimes, people just need us to listen, try to understand their hurts and pains, and encourage them not to give up. I know a thing or two about needing a messenger of hope.

Growing up in the country brought the well-chronicled experience of a boy and his dog; in my case, it was with my collie named Duff. Collies are very intelligent, easy to train, and have a natural affection for people. We had hours of adventure romping through the fields, exploring the woods, or wading in the creeks of our farm. Then, when I was nine, I experienced one of the most traumatic events of my young life. Whenever we would feed the cattle in the morning or check on them at any other time, Duff would want to ride along. He would hear the old Willy's Jeep fire up and come running. His spot was sitting right between my dad and me, where he could look out the windshield.

One evening, the cows had gotten out, so we had to drive down the public road to put them back in and repair the fence. To complete the job, Daddy had to go back for a tool, so we jumped into the Jeep and headed back home. Duff was out in the fields, but when he heard the Jeep start up, he came racing after us. We started down the road, and just as Duff came out of the field, a car came along and ran over him. I still remember my guttural sob of anguish as I watched my dad pick his lifeless body off the road. Nothing could assuage that pain. Not even the Irish Setter puppy Daddy brought home the next day. I do remember the efforts both of my parents extended to comfort me, and they were messengers of hope with their listening and care.

Sometimes, our customers just need a messenger of hope before any problem can be solved. If we are going to do that, we need to be able to listen to their problems and show genuine care. We cannot be good problem-solvers if we don't first take the time to understand the customers. We have to do it all with Unwavering Positivity because it makes the process better and more effective for everyone involved. This is not a pie-in-the-sky value for us: we are in the customer care and problem-solving business and lean into that responsibility with genuine excitement.

One of our highest-performing salespeople over the last four years is Tamara. Tamara had no previous background in sales, having worked in the fast-food business and retail and as a dog walker before joining Easy Step. Initially, she struggled to adapt to the arch supports and was close to giving up. Then, one day, she put on her shoes with her arch supports and discovered the pain she had struggled with for so long was gone. Her success in sales is due to her being a relentless problem solver. She is so passionate about helping people that she will not give up until she finds a solution. Her customers perceive this commitment to helping them, which creates a high level of trust, which is the key ingredient in selling.

Life brings unfairness, loss, and pain, whether it is the loss of a collie or some other hurt. Our customers are often "weary with anxiety," and it is a blessing to offer Unwavering Positivity and provide true hope. Whether you run a hardware store or a coffee shop or offer sophisticated technology solutions to customers, care and concern for their problems can infuse significant value into the overall offering.

Systems to Reinforce Unwavering Positivity

Unwavering Positivity is defined as: "Expressing joy in being a problem-solver, a collaborator in wellness, a proponent of enjoying life. In a world weary with anxiety, we choose to be messengers of hope." Here, the crucial phrase is problem-solver—because we want problem-solving to be a foundational part of our company culture at all levels. To be a problem-solver, the employee has to have the desire, the competence, and the capacity.

Problem-Solving Focus: Since Unwavering Positivity is much more than a cheery disposition, we frame everything we do in terms of what problems we can solve for others and how we can help. Doing this takes the concept of "positivity" out of the air and brings it down to earth. The value of a company to its customers and community is determined by the significance of the problems it tackles and the efficacy of its products and services—the more challenging the problem, the greater the opportunity to transform the experience of a customer.

Transforming Obstacles: When a goal is established, challenges or obstacles will inevitably arise. By embracing Unwavering Positivity, our team members view an obstacle as containing an embedded strategy to achieve the goal. In sales, handling an objection with care and concern is an example. Old-school selling teaches manipulation and overpowering the customer with the force of argument or personality. When a customer raises an objection, asking a question with the attitude of "expressing joy in being a problem-solver, a collaborator in wellness, a proponent of enjoying life" goes a long way to a successful sale.

"Persistent Diligence"

Having a champion's commitment to excellence. We embrace the truth of the timeless proverb: "Slack habits and sloppy work are as bad as vandalism (Proverbs 18:9, NKJV)."

"Having a champion's commitment to excellence" sounds warm and inviting until we have insight into the champion's incredible commitment. In the context of athletic champions, many people probably thought they were crazy before they achieved what they did—as they relentlessly pursued their workouts and their practices, got up early and trained in the rain, snow, and blistering sun, or repeated boring exercises over and over and over again. Through all of that action, the champions knew who they were and what they were doing, and they never got confused; *that* is what makes a champion. In addition to the physical commitment of a champion, there is also the mental and emotional discipline they bring. I have observed elite athletes and how they handle correction from a coach both at practice or in a game where large audiences are watching. It requires great humility to be accountable to a high standard, especially when the player knows they have extraordinary talent. All of these things are what defines a true champion.

Excellence is something we should all strive for in business, but growth can be an existential threat to excellence. Bigger numbers, new initiatives, and wider scopes of operation can all be siren songs that shipwreck excellence. Only through relentless intentionality and fierce determination will we sustain excellence in a high-growth environment. At Easy Step, it's a question we're always asking ourselves: do we have that relentless intentionality and fierce determination?

The second part of this value is a focus on opportunity cost, as one of the most underreported costs in business is that of missed opportunities. You may not see it on a financial statement, but it is one of the biggest expenses that we all have. We teach this value by focusing on the proverb, "Slack habits and sloppy work are as bad as vandalism." Most of us have a visceral reaction to vandalism and the wanton destruction of property for no reason. Seeing someone throw a brick through the store's front window would likely make us angry. Yet, in every business I have been a part of, "slack habits and sloppy work" are as costly as vandalism and sometimes exponentially more expensive.

At Easy Step, we have regular opportunities to introduce customers to our life-changing products, and when everything clicks, strong performance follows. Yet sometimes, they don't make a purchase because maybe our store wasn't staffed properly, our marketing did not work right, or we didn't have an effective sales training program in place. Maybe we made promises to customers and didn't follow through, leaving the customers thinking that we were in a game with the wrong intentions or scamming them out of money. As Henry Cloud says, "Follow the pain, make a rule." The rule becomes part of the process, and the process must be followed with Persistent Diligence.

Persistent Diligence is closely tied to Radical Integrity. The value of steely discipline gives practical relevance to the culture. There are aspects of business that require what I call "air traffic control accuracy." Persistent Diligence produces a thorough process, rigorous practice, attention to that process, and alignment with the reporting metrics. Successful surgery, safe takeoffs and landings, treasured wedding photography, and that exquisite meal celebrating a life milestone all hinge on Persistent Diligence.

Systems to Reinforce Persistent Diligence

Persistent Diligence is "Having a champion's commitment to excellence. We embrace the truth of the timeless proverb: "Slack habits and sloppy work are as bad as vandalism." Approaching our work with the dedication of a champion instills the discipline to do hard things with a vision.

Commitment to Excellence: We consider the pursuit of excellence essential to what we do, akin to a champion's dedication to achieving a challenging goal. You may have picked up by now that I am a Virginia Cavalier sports fan. Hopefully, you will keep reading if you are a Duke, Kentucky, or Michigan fan. In 2018, the Virginia Cavaliers were the #1 overall seed in the NCAA tournament—but they lost to the #16 seed, University of Maryland, Baltimore County (UMBC), in the first round. It was a historic, humiliating loss, but the team knew they couldn't give up or accept it. To motivate his team from hopelessness to celebration, Coach

Tony Bennett shared a TEDx talk by Donald Davis. "It's this idea that adversity, 'if you learn to use it right, it can buy you a ticket to a place you wouldn't have gone any other way.'" Following his advice to the letter, the team didn't get discouraged or engage in self-pity, and the following year, they won an NCAA Championship. To me, that is the commitment and dedication we're describing when it comes to pursuing excellence, and it informs how we think about everything that goes into creating it.

Growth vs. Excellence: Often, businesses can think of growth exclusively in monetary or mathematical terms. With this outlook, growth is defined simply as more of something: more sales, more stores, more profit, and so on. Though growth is an important value in itself, pursuing growth at any cost isn't something we do, particularly because growth can come at the cost of excellence. When a company grows, that growth often adds complexity: there are more employees to align with the leadership's vision, more customer stories to understand before making a sale, and, in some ways, exponentially more chances to "get it wrong." By seeing growth as a potential threat to excellence rather than an imperative all on its own, we find a pace and strategy for growth that works with our values rather than against them. As we've learned over time through trial and error, excellence can only be maintained through intentionality and determination, not by simply adding "more" wherever we can.

Opportunity Cost: The reduction of missed opportunities is an essential part of true excellence. By simply excusing mistakes or even accepting "good" outcomes at face value, we either forgive or congratulate ourselves prematurely, missing the opportunity for the truly "great." Instead of getting comfortable or coasting on our successes, we take time for extra self-reflection to fuel continual improvement and better resilience, which are the true markers of excellence.

Moving from values to processes, as we've done above, can help businesses take their vision and mission and make them concrete and actionable. Altogether, enforcing those processes is character-driven leadership, reinforcing a character-driven culture. Culture, like character, is central, not peripheral, to business success. It needs to be actively managed, monitored, and cultivated, similar to financial accounts. Though it might start with leadership, leadership can only create the environment; willing and enthusiastic participants have to be the ones to fill it.

The Power of Values in Business and Leadership

Values can be both the most specific and the most abstract part of a business. They are a critical daily responsibility of business leaders, and often, the best measure of how effectively a leader practices these values comes from the feedback of those around them. Our character has the power to impact people even during our absence. My youngest son, Jentry, likes to share a story about my time in the moving industry that illustrates this point:

> I had the unique opportunity to work in the moving industry after my dad had left the business. He spent over 25 years in the industry and left a successful legacy of working with some of the top brands in the corporate world as well as some of the biggest names in the country. As I got to know people in the industry and sat in on workshops with his former competitors, leaders of companies would talk about integrity in the business. During one particular meeting, the CEO of a large moving company was discussing the ethics of the business, and he kind of lightheartedly said, "Would Jonathan Cotten do this if he were here?" It got a few chuckles from others in the room

because there was a meaning behind the statement. People knew about Jonathan's integrity in the business. He was never a high-level executive—one might say he was just a regular sales guy—but he expected a high level of integrity not only from his coworkers but also from his own customers. Even if you are not the leader of a company, your character can manifest itself for many years to come. This type of character can make you a leader in a company, with or without the title.

Jentry and I have worked together in many different environments since he was a young boy, so his kind words are very humbling. He also has plenty of stories about his dad's faults that he could have shared, so this is an example of grace, and all glory goes to God. The point is that you do not have to be an owner or CEO to lead with character. John Maxwell has rightly pointed out that "leadership is influence," and if we build influence on character, it will have power in our presence or absence.

One of the challenges as a leader who focuses on character is helping people on different teams understand who they are and decode their "why" for what they are doing. All of our "whys" can be somewhat different, which is okay—but we must all share the *motivation* to enter the public arena to fulfill our calling and purpose, even if that motivation always comes from an internal, private source.

When motivation comes from the right source, it significantly changes the way a company runs. Making a business work requires staying centered and grounded: understanding the numbers, managing people according to them, and keeping everyone aligned. But it's also necessary to go beyond the numbers and data because managing the mindset of everyone involved is one of the hardest challenges.

At Easy Step Enterprises, we try to do that by developing a "winning mentality" in our employees and helping them get as many "wins" as possible. Through getting many wins, they build confidence through small victories, and things get better and better. Dan Sullivan says, "The number one thing an entrepreneur must protect is their confidence." Any person in business who receives a significant percentage of their pay in bonuses, commissions, or incentive pay is a mini-entrepreneur because they are constantly risking their own paycheck and bonuses. For those people, then, protecting their confidence is also a priority.

Victor Frankl, holocaust survivor and author of *Man's Search for Meaning*, quotes Friedrich Nietzsche about how people can accomplish such impossible things: "You can bear any 'how' if you have a sufficient 'why.'" We follow that wisdom when we challenge our sales teams by explaining that focusing *only* on numbers makes for a very empty "why." When they fully embrace the beauty of our business, they make a significant income *while* helping people. With that dynamic mix of metrics and helping others, we all can achieve the greatest success.

As we think about the ideals we assent to, it is good to ask, "Am I truly aligned with my ideals in practice?" If we say things like, "I love my neighbor," what would that actually look like if we were fully in alignment with it? In what ways would our behavior have to change?

In a business context, when I think about Easy Step's vision, mission, and values, I ask myself: do my customers, fellow employees, and community see our values practiced with consistency in my life? To stay accountable to the standards I ask of others, I make it a practice to remind myself of these questions every day. At times, it is hard for me to realize that what I may describe as simply being passionate, ambitious, and action-oriented can come off to others as being rude, self-serving, and lacking thoughtfulness. Ouch! When that is the feedback, it is time for more recalibration of the Values, which is an ongoing process. As leaders who receive a lot of recognition, a verse that can apply here refers to those who are arrogant by saying, "In their own eyes they flatter themselves too much to detect or hate their own sin" (Psalm 36:2). We need truthtellers around us and regular reflection on our personal alignment with our Values.

Defining Your Own Values: Questions for Reflection

If a vision statement is the north star or GPS and the mission statement is the fuel in the tank, a company's values are its flanges on the track that keep the company trained on the course. A leader of a company has to know where they are going and have fuel in the tank to get there, but they also need guiding principles to ensure they don't get off track. Values have to speak to everyone in clear, ringing terms. They must be specific to be actionable yet inclusive enough so that all departments, positions, and people are reached.

• • •

To begin thinking about what values your company will uphold, it helps to think of values as covering four broad areas:

1) **Integrity:** *The ability to accurately assess our own character, to have healthy relationships with others, and to be held accountable for our actions.*

2) **Desire:** *The innate drive and internal motivation to accomplish goals.*

3) **Care:** *Valuing the impact we have on others, whether colleagues, customers, or the community.*

4) **Commitment:** *Being devoted to achieving maximum performance that is consistent with our abilities and position.*

Whenever I speak to new employees, I tell them the two essential elements they must possess on day one are baseline integrity and desire (the saying my dad always used to say related to desire was, "You can't push a rope."). While all of our values are crucial as well, integrity and desire come first, and the other values can be developed over time and reinforced through a company's culture. This is important, as truly understanding what culture you have requires a minimum of six months (often up to a year). Much of that time should be spent doing a deep dive into values, all to help employees understand that they are not accessories to the business but are actually vital, core drivers of business.

• • •

While a company's values must be present in all employees and at all levels, establishing clear values clearly and closely monitoring them is a job for the leadership. With this in mind, here are some things for business leaders to consider:

1) How do you approach management, and what is your personal leadership style? How does it complement or come in conflict with the company's values and overall culture? What adjustments could you make if things aren't working as well as they could, and which stakeholders are most important to talk to to get the information you need to make the change?

2) How do you (or will you) know when and where your leadership style is serving you and your organization? What metrics do you currently have in place to measure leadership success, and how might they be adjusted?

3) Related to the four areas of values mentioned above, what tools will you use to screen for the first two crucial qualities of integrity and desire in your hiring process? What processes are in place, and how might you adjust them?

• • •

For further reading, I'll include a few resources that have helped me tremendously because my perspective on integrity was influenced dramatically by two people:

1) *Mick and Sandy Lee, founders of Plus Relocation Services, established Radical Integrity as a value at their company. I had the opportunity to see it play out successfully in day-to-day business with Susan Benevides and Joe Benevides, who continue to emphasize a values-driven culture. Reading about their approach to culture is sure to help illustrate what operating with values and integrity looks like: https://PlusRelocation.com/culture/. (I did tell the leaders of Plus that imitation is the sincerest form of flattery. I could not think of a better phrase than Radical Integrity, so I risked being guilty of plagiarism in adopting this from them.)*

2) *Dr. Henry Cloud's book* Integrity *is also a great resource, stressing the importance of starting with introspection as opposed to looking only at the outward expression of honesty or truthfulness. Dr. Cloud's book was a major influence on me when writing the description of Radical Integrity.*

5

Playing Cultural Defense: Lessons from a National Champion

rowing up in Atlantic Coast Conference (ACC) basketball country, I loved college basketball from a young age.
The close proximity to Charlottesville fostered an alle-
giance to the University of Virginia and its program, even
though I never attended as a student. When I went into business, I naturally explored the opportunity to sponsor Virginia
athletics, particularly basketball.

In the context of athletics (though also in life and business), a coach can take the great character of their athletes

and hone it into something truly excellent—which is where organizational high character starts to emerge. More than just athletic development, some of the greatest coaches have seen the value of character development as being an essential component to long-term individual and team success. John Wooden of UCLA, Dean Smith of North Carolina, and more recently, Scott Drew of Baylor are examples of men's championship college basketball coaches who emphasized culture and the character of their athletes and not just their performance on the court. The late, legendary Pat Summitt on the women's basketball side, as well as South Carolina's current Championship coach, Dawn Staley, are also outstanding examples of coaches who have used basketball as a platform to infuse lifelong lessons into their players.

In the case of UVA, and as a longtime fan of their basketball program myself, I have long admired Tony Bennett's commitment to developing character on an individual and team level. He is known for his calm, kind demeanor in games, yet a champion is going to have intensity, and Coach Bennett is no exception. I have watched him in practice relentlessly emphasize a certain play or discipline, usually on the defensive side of the court, and also watched his players accept the correction or instruction without taking it personally. As Isaac McKneely, a star UVA guard, described it to me, "Coach Bennett never attacks you personally, but practice is often intense because he is not going to accept mediocre commitment."

Not everyone admires Tony's approach, given that it is highly centered on defense, as opposed to a fast-paced offense approach. Yet the emphasis on the fundamentals of basketball reflects the priority he places on things such as discipline, integrity, and character.

Tony Bennett's approach has been well chronicled, first with derisive criticism after UVA was upset as the #1 overall seed by #16 UMBC in the 2018 NCAA Men's Basketball

Tournament. For some, this loss was prima facie evidence that prioritizing character and values could not coexist with the cold-blooded competitiveness needed to win at the highest level. However, in storybook fashion, UVA came back in 2019 to claim the National Championship, and this time, the praise was effusive. Culture and values do matter, after all, and their contribution to Virginia's National Championship was obvious.

In January 2020, I had my first meeting and visit with Tony Bennett at his "Coach's Corner" broadcast in Charlottesville. My daughter Kayla was with me, and in their conversation, she shared her health journey and decision to withdraw from college due to her condition. The next day, I received an email from Dave Koehn, the UVA play-by-play broadcaster. Tony wanted to know more about Kayla and wondered if I would be willing to share. I responded with a summary of her health odyssey of battling mitochondrial disease since age 15, her numerous ER visits, hospital admissions, and five sepsis infections.

The following Saturday, I had courtside seats for the UVA game against Syracuse, which was a first for me. I invited Kayla, and we arrived early for the game. As we waited, the associate athletics director for men's basketball, Ronnie Wideman, came over and introduced himself. He said Tony wanted to visit with us before the game. Thinking maybe Coach wanted to say a few words in the tunnel as he came out to the court, I readily agreed. About 20 minutes later, Ronnie led us to an elevator that took us to Tony Bennett's office. As we entered, he introduced us to George Morris, FCA chaplain for Virginia Basketball. We sat down, and Coach Bennett said, "Kayla, after I met you the other night, I went home and told Laurel, my wife, that I met a sister in Christ who has had a remarkable journey. We may never see each other again in this life, but I wanted to invite you and your dad up here to pray."

As I sat with tears streaming down my face, George Morris, in his deep, sonorous voice, led us in a sincere, heartfelt prayer. Tip-off was just 30 minutes away, and here, the reigning NCAA Championship coach was taking the time to visit and pray for someone he hardly knew. True, The Good Feet Store was a sponsor, but not at anywhere near the level that would warrant this type of attention.

As I have been able to observe Tony over the years and watch him in practice, coach games against Top 10 opponents, and under the intense scrutiny of media and fans, it has been confirmed that character counts and building programs on a solid foundation of values is prudent for long-term success. Tony's father, Coach Dick Bennett, created five pillars that are the backbone of the program, and Tony has carried them into his coaching career:

Tony Bennett's Five Pillars of Success:

- Humility: Know who we are.
- Passion: Do not be lukewarm.
- Unity: Do not divide our house.
- Servanthood: Makes teams better.
- Thankfulness: Learn from each circumstance.

Recently, Coach Bennett sat down with me to elaborate on these pillars and what they mean to him and his team:

The missionary Jim Elliot said, "He is no fool who gives what he cannot keep to gain that which he cannot lose." All of us have been given so many gifts, and when you share them, you gain something of everlasting value. When you treat people well and use your values to serve them, you gain something in the long run. Those are the things that go far beyond the immediate. There is so much power in loving people, treating them well, and doing it with joy.

Any good program starts with solid beliefs. They don't have to be biblical pillars, but they must be something that you own, believe in, and that matters to you. They must be concepts you can articulate well yet are more than mere lip service, words on the wall, or a bookmark. You must believe them.

The values of our program can be traced back to my father. As a man of faith and a basketball coach, he wanted his faith to play out in his vocation. So, he studied the scriptures and asked, "What would make for a really good basketball team?" Through his studies, he settled on certain character traits that he thought would help with both the tactical stuff on the court and how you do life off the court.

His starting point was humility, the first pillar. In any industry, if you don't have an understanding of your identity, you'll get chewed up and spit out. You need to be able to look at yourself in the mirror and say, "Alright, who am I? What do I want my business and my leadership to look like? What are the important things?" Once you find the answer, you need to stick to that. Scripturally, humility is a position of not thinking too highly of yourself and not thinking too lowly of yourself. It is having sober judgment.

These pillars that my father came up with are the teachings of Christ, the things He taught to His disciples. In the leadership book Good to Great by Jim Collins, he identifies what separates certain leaders. The number one trait was humility. Those who had a proper view of themselves led from a position of strength, not weakness. Start with a humble spirit and identity. There is always something you can learn. You need a willingness to look at yourself with humility and ask, "What do I need to become better in this area? What am I lacking?" Embrace that and move in those directions. I find it ironic that if you're not humble, you will be humbled. Pride goes before the fall. "Those who exalt themselves will be humbled. Those who humble themselves will be exalted." If we are not humble, it shows.

It also shows when we're not living out our second pillar, passion. If you aren't passionate, if you don't love what you do, it will show. If we don't have a fierce commitment to doing our work well, we're lukewarm. When that is the case, usually, we'll fail.

Ultimately, we win or lose as a team. That is why our third pillar, unity, is critical. We struggle if we're not unified, and things become more about "me" and not about us. Everything gets exposed in the pressure of the game; it's a great teacher. It can be easy for players who always start or get a lot of attention from the media to think of themselves too highly. It can also be easy for players who sit on the bench to think they are not as valuable to the team as they really are. It takes intentionality to be united as a team.

If we are not willing to serve each other on and off the court, our self-centeredness will be evident. We will seem entitled. Servanthood is one of my favorite pillars because it is so rewarding to watch the guys truly care for each other in a way that goes far beyond the typical teammate relationship.

Thankfulness is not just something you should have when things are going well. You need to be able to look at the hard times and ask yourself, "What did it teach me?" I am thankful for what I am learning.

While all of them get tested at different times, our five pillars have stayed the same. They have grown in my mind. I have lived them through all different kinds of experiences, and I understand them on a much deeper level. Even in my studies of scripture, different things continue to come to light. You see the value in them, how they work, and how they rely on each other.

The pillars are like your north star, and we try to recruit to those. We try to coach those. Usually, you can point to one, two, or multiple of these pillars in yourself or your program when things are not going well and find that something is off. You can say, "Hey, look, are we truly being these things?" Sometimes, they are more valuable in the hard times of adversity than in the good times.

When it comes to values, no one has them all down perfectly. Everyone is a work in progress. I love what Billy Graham's wife put on her tomb, "Construction finished." We are all a work in progress until the day we are made whole with our Lord and Savior, if that is your faith. While you can't expect anyone to have them all, you can expect everyone on your team to respect, honor, and practice them.

When we recruit and hire, we look for people with whom we can truly experience loss and adversity. Those are the ones who will apply the pillars to their lives and be good teammates.

Sometimes, you don't fully know someone's character if you haven't assessed how they are when things go wrong. How are these people when the rubber meets the road? How do they react when they get injured, aren't playing as much, or life just gets hard? When you compromise values for talent, this is when you can tell and start to regret it. Before recruiting or hiring someone, I will typically go to a few of their close friends or family and say, "Tell me about this person. What are they like when it's going bad? How do they respond to their teammates?"

Leaders will have hard decisions to make. I struggle because I don't like letting the players down. I know how passionate they are and how much they want to play. However, you have to do what you think is best to help your program in the right way. And that is extremely challenging for young men who work so hard and want it so badly. I struggle when I have to look them in the eye and say, "This isn't your time," or "You have to wait." It's hard to be good. It's difficult to be patient.

While there are a few cases where players see success right away, that is not typical. There is a process that you can't bypass. You have to work. You have to put in the daily deposits and be patient. It's like the Bible verse that says to not grow weary in doing good, but in due time you will reap a harvest (Galatians 6:9). Sometimes, you have to shift what their definition of success looks like. Players think they will come in and be the star because they come from a team where they were the star. However, with so many good players here, some must wait their turn. They just might have to be great in practice and earn their time.

Culture screams, "If it doesn't happen right away, boom! Go somewhere else." I think the willingness to humble themselves, honor the process, take what they can get, and trust that you have their best interest at heart builds character. There will be a difficult road to get to where they want. That is just reality. Will you stay patient? Will you buy in and then work like crazy to get better? Sustaining our culture has become more difficult because of the way college sports allow players to transfer right away. It used to be the best thing for them to go through those valleys and come out more mature. So many don't want to go through that, but it is the ones who are willing to fight and stay patient that come out on top.

There are areas where you have to be willing to adapt and adjust. There are other areas where you should not be willing to compromise. You need to hold on to the things that matter, to the pillars and values. You can't control what the following year holds. Maybe you don't build programs in three or four years. Perhaps it's every year or two at a time. It doesn't change how you work with your young men, how you treat them, or how you pour into them.

We are always judged at the end on how successful we are, but I think when you get in the business of compromising what matters to you, you are on a slippery slope. I think not much has changed regarding what we value, what we have instilled in our players, and how we try to play the game. Yes, there are new trends and little adjustments, but the core stays the same. I think that's the strength of a well-built house, one that is built on the right foundation and values.

That's my greatest fear in this whole new shift in college basketball. It's become all transactional. So, you try to go against the grain and be transformational, honor what your culture is, honor your pillars, and still compete in a way that gives you a chance. Can you? I don't know. It's a whole different world. Time will tell. I think, yes, it's entertainment. Yes, the product on the floor is probably better because of things that have happened. But what's being lost is the best stuff that happened to young people, this whole process of amateur college athletics. Let's not sacrifice the things that are most important in a vain attempt to gain things we cannot keep anyway.

Tony Bennett's words resonate with me on a deep level. In business, it can be so easy to be trapped in transactional thinking, where every decision has to be processed through a decision matrix of "What's our ROI"? There are times to tap the brakes on the immediate ROI discussion and invest a little more with a developing new employee, go the extra mile to ensure a customer is satisfied, or staff the store with an extra employee to ensure everyone's safety. Make decisions first based on alignment with values, and if the boxes are checked there, then you can pursue ROI with much more clarity. The more vibrant and distinct a culture becomes, the more magnetic power it has to employees, customers, and all other like-minded stakeholders.

Challenges will come in business just as they currently exist in college athletics. In the world of college athletics, with the transfer portal and highly transactional Name, Image, and Likeness (NIL) deals, a program centered around character, integrity, and values is at a competitive disadvantage. Yet, the commitment to these values is a strategic advantage, offering a clear outlier for those who have similar commitments. There are some things that money cannot buy, and in athletics and business, vibrant culture is one of those things.

As a recruiting magnet alone, a dynamic and consistent culture is a powerful force. When there is a bias to want to wear a jersey with the name of an institution that values honor or to be known as an employee of an organization with an excellent reputation in the community, you are no longer engaged in simply a bidding war for talent. Throughout Tony Bennett's tenure as a head coach at Virginia, there has been a minimal amount of off-court drama or distraction with his players. The team's chemistry and locker room cohesion have been major contributors to his .728 winning percentage during his time at Virginia.

In July 2021, the Supreme Court cleared the way for college athletes to be paid for their NIL. That fall, we signed an NIL agreement with Kihei Clark, a junior point guard for UVA, with an NCAA National Championship on his resume. The basis for selecting Kihei, however, was first due to the character that he had demonstrated throughout his college career. Basketball is an intimate spectator sport, where due to the location of the court and the lack of helmets or other gear, the reactions and expressions of the athlete are clearly seen. Kihei had unflappable poise as a player, which led to the signature play of his college career. As a first-year player, during the final minutes of the Regional Finals against Purdue, he tracked down a tipped ball. He delivered a pass with pinpoint accuracy to Mamadi Diakite, who then tied the game, forcing overtime, with Virginia advancing to the Final Four. Kihei also maintained a sterling reputation on and off the court throughout his college career.

An interesting note about Kihei is that he was not pursued by many Division I schools out of high school. In a highly competitive landscape, with the world's best athletes vying for roster spots, how does a lightly recruited, first-year guard find himself dribbling the ball up the court at the National Championship in Minneapolis? Character is a significant part of the answer. For Coach Bennett, a player who embraces his five pillars of Humility, Passion, Unity, Servanthood, and Thankfulness is equipped with the foundation for success. Kihei is a classic example of this principle.

Later, we expanded our NIL program to include Jayden Gardner, a 6'7" forward who had transferred to Virginia from East Carolina University. Like Kihei, Jayden was exemplary in his conduct and a joy to work with. When a call or play would not go his way, the immediate frustration on his face would quickly dissipate into a smile. A very unusual attribute for a highly competitive athlete, I believe, in Jayden's case, is a demonstration of his faith in Christ and his desire to glorify God in his athletic career. The ability to establish NIL agreements with players has given me insight into the type of players Tony Bennett recruits, and it validates even further the value of the foundation of character.

When I consider our growth as a company, the only way it has been possible has been by having high-character employees who have made unbelievable contributions over the years. Tony Bennett says that he recruits players that he can lose with, which I translate in business as having employees that you trust, have high competency, and enjoy working with, even while you are still working to be profitable. With a great culture and the right strategy, EBIDTA results will come in time, provided you have the right people of character who are all-in on the vision.

Laura Worosher, who has been such a vital help to me in so many initiatives over the years, has often said, "I will work for jellybeans," which indicates two things: one, her loyal commitment, and two, her love of jellybeans. This reflects the Business of Character, where the motivation is not the pot of gold at the end of the rainbow but rather the fulfillment of working with purpose along the way. "Recruiting players you can lose with" and "working for jellybeans" are two ways to express the same thought. Everyone understands the "why," shared convictions guide them, and they have faith that, over time, these commitments will yield satisfying, sustainable success.

Note: Shortly before this book went to press, on October 17, 2024, Tony Bennett announced his retirement from coaching basketball at The University of Virginia. During his press conference, Coach Bennett said, "I don't do anything without going to the Lord in prayer and seeking Him. Again, when you feel something impressed upon your heart and spirit, and you're faithful about it, I think that's a significant part."

He also said, "When you know in your heart it's time, it's time. Will I miss the game? Do I love the game? Absolutely, but I don't think I'm equipped in this new way to coach, and it's a disservice if you keep doing that. I'm very sure that this is the right step, and I wish I could have gone longer, I really do, but it was time, and I wouldn't have done it if I didn't think we had the right group of young men and the right staff to lead them forward in this way."

Even in his retirement press conference, he displayed the same unyielding commitment to values and integrity. Of all the people I have known who would be recognized as a nationally acclaimed celebrity, Coach Bennett embodies a leader committed to the Business of Character. Examples like his inspire me in my journey.

6

Character, Culture, and Family: Living an Integrated Life

Hold on to instruction, do not let it go;
guard it well for it is your life.
—*Proverbs 4:13*

Learning Valuable Lessons in Childhood

The childhood memory of that beautiful farm in Crozet, Virginia, is indelibly imprinted on my mind. There was my dad on a weekday in 1975, driving a tractor around and bush-hogging the pasture. It was unusual because he was a businessman with a busy schedule. He would leave first thing in the morning, jump into his car, and be gone until evening. Whenever he came home, I would hide behind a tree; as a little kid, his football player frame, impeccable suit, and stern look behind the sunglasses were intimidating.

Watching him on the tractor that day, I tossed around a new word in my mind: bankruptcy. That was what he was trying to process. The word would take on profound meaning after months of legal proceedings, all leading to saying goodbye to our 5,000-square-foot house on 70 acres with a three-story barn nestled against the Blue Ridge Mountains. Our idyllic home and even a steer I was raising were all liquidated. Now, we had to get used to a 1,300-square-foot rental house.

The financial change was bad enough, but soon, I saw Daddy serve as a public example of what not to do in business. I have seen firsthand how churches and religious groups can do incredible harm as well as good. Ours decided that bankruptcy was a major character defect that reflected greed, so he was excommunicated for a period of time shortly after going through financial troubles. In the eyes of the church, Claude Cotten had to be broken to teach him and everyone else a lesson.

Even so, resiliency was a character trait deeply ingrained in him due to living through the Depression in West Texas, and he set out quickly to meet the challenge at hand. While I admired his determination, as a young boy, I had a first-row seat in the "Reasons to Never Go Into Business" seminar— and seeing what he went through is maybe why it took me until I was 49 to try it myself.

One of the incredible blessings in my life is never questioning that Daddy and Mother loved me, loved each other, and were faithful to one another for over 60 years in marriage. One of my favorite work activities growing up was going out with Daddy early in the morning before school, in the snow, getting into our 1950s Willy's Jeep with a trailer, and tossing hay off the trailer to feed the cows. At the time, for both of us, it did not seem like a significant event, yet those memories last a lifetime.

I was once at a work event and went over to say hello to some other attendees. As I got close, the man nearest the front said, "Are you any relation to Claude Cotten?" I told him that Claude was my dad. He went on to tell me that he bought a house in Woodbrook in Charlottesville, Virginia, in 1968 that my dad had built and then raved about how well the house had been constructed. This came as no surprise because "good 'nuff" was not something my dad subscribed to. He would talk about (and show me) the right way to frame a wall, install finish trim, and even handle a shovel of gravel (and since the only thing I was able to get down was the shoveling, I eventually became motivated to learn sales). It was so rewarding to meet someone still talking about the excellence my dad pursued in craftsmanship 55 years later.

I still remember a moment many years ago at a home show in the old Armory building in Charlottesville. My dad had a booth for a franchise he had recently acquired from New England Log Homes. He was selling packages for log homes that people would buy, and he asked me to help him. I had already decided I was not interested in the operations side of the construction industry. Wearing a nail bag with a framing hammer was not my gig, even though my dad, uncles, and brothers all enjoyed it. But now, I was in this booth, engaging people as they came by. At 15 years old, I was having fun. Many years later, when I was exposed to the Strategic Coach concept of Unique Ability®, I thought back on this moment. While I was not made for framing walls, I quickly found my rhythm when I was talking to prospective customers about how a home was built.

I also learned lessons from watching Dad struggle and fail to fully integrate his faith, his family, and his work. He was ambitious, which caused him to take on too much debt and enter into inadvisable ventures. Dad was so driven that he would often run over people in the heat of the moment with a dominance that would cause deep resentment. As a result, he was sometimes conflicted and out of alignment with his faith, which had authenticity, and his love for his family, which was also very real. I observed this, and once I got married, with Kathryn's support and encouragement, I wanted things to be different.

Integrating Work into Marriage and Fatherhood

After 40 years of marriage, I look back and have an over-whelming sense of immense joy and gratitude for my family. We have a treasure chest of memories of the quality and quantity of time spent together, living life, laughing, crying, studying, playing, and working. Working together at home and then working with me as my boys began to get older. Due to her health condition, my opportunity to do this with Kayla was limited, but even so, we enjoyed times working together.

Keep in mind that my kids did not have much of an example of a skilled craftsman to follow. They learned quickly that their dad would get frustrated and demonstrate his ineptitude if a given task required much mechanical ability. But when it came to mowing a big lawn, raking leaves, cutting up trees with my Stihl chainsaw, and then splitting and stacking the firewood, there were plenty of lessons to learn. Any young person can benefit from the value of sweating while working. It is different from practicing and playing a sport and requires a different kind of endurance.

These are some of the reasons that I resist the phrase "work/life balance." Implicit in that phrase is that "life" is excluded from "work" and vice versa. When our families can enter into our work world, the lessons and benefits multiply. From the time they were very young, my boys would expect that, more often than not, we would work on Saturdays, either at home or they would go with me to work. The entire family would frequently travel with me on business trips, and they would hear me on business calls or recount what happened on an appointment. In addition to traveling to New York, Philadelphia, Atlanta, and other cities on longer trips, they would regularly accompany me to Washington, DC, and I would drop them off at the Smithsonian or the Capitol, where they would sit in the gallery and watch the House or Senate proceedings. It is quite a civics lesson to observe impeachment proceedings against a sitting president in real-time, and it would have never happened if they were not along for a business trip.

One of the great blessings in my work journey and my entrepreneurial journey has been the ability to engage my family in my work. It is not always possible in every work environment, yet with thought, we can invite our families into what can be an excellent life development opportunity for them and a relational development opportunity for everyone. Yes, the dangers are there, and the failures are well documented, but a tremendous upside also exists. Sometimes, people distance their families, especially their children, from work. Throughout their childhood, our children met my bosses, my colleagues, and often, my customers. My work colleagues enjoyed it, and it helped my kids on multiple levels.

First, it gave a lot more context to Dad going to work, and they felt more involved in it; it wasn't something only I was doing that they were detached from. Second, there were valuable lessons in exposing my kids to different work environments. Not only did they get more opportunities to relate to adults, but they learned lessons that they could never have learned in a lecture or class. Third, as they started to formulate their own thoughts on work, it gave them the opportunity to see what other people did in a work setting.

I realize those experiences may be unique to our family, and if you work in an oil refinery, it may be tough to have a "bring your kids to work" day. Yet, when children can see that we have joy in our work, depth in our relationships with our work colleagues, and mutual respect with our customers, it will leave a lifelong impact. This is an integrated life where character, culture, and family can live harmoniously. It is not the zero-sum game type of thinking where a gain for work means an automatic loss for the family. Or where quality family time can only exist if we have small business goals. When our family sees us in the work arena, living out our faith and character imperfectly yet with intentionality, it will provide an essential life framework.

Family and the Journey of an Entrepreneur

This foundation of an approach to character, family, and work has paid huge dividends in our business. As our oldest, Joseph was the guinea pig as I embarked on my parenting journey as a 20-year-old father. He endured my efforts to implement the "101 Things a Child Needs to Be Taught," with 96 of them being inconsequential when five would have sufficed. Yet one of the saving graces in our relationship was the time we spent together, often in work activities. He was able to get an early glimpse of what the work world is like and progressively participate with me in it instead of waiting until college was over to find out. He set a great example for his siblings by being diligent and purposeful both in his work and at college, and that influence continues to bless us. Joseph does not work actively in the business today, but he has contributed significantly by helping with our insurance needs through his insurance agency as we have continued to grow.

Jarrin, our second son, chose the electrical field as a teenager rather than pursue college. I was disappointed in this choice because he had always done well in school and was academically inclined. Yet, I also believed it was vital for him to make his own choice, which he did, and he rose to the point of starting to attain the status of master electrician. At the time, I was working for Plus Relocation Services, and there was a need for a support person to research corporations for those of us in major account sales. I mentioned Jarrin as a candidate, and they hired him, which led to another experience of working with my sons. When I left Plus Relocation to buy the store and go into business, Jarrin entered training to go into corporate sales. He began succeeding and ultimately closed the largest corporate client in their 40+ year corporate history. By this time, he and his wife Courtney had four children, and the extensive travel conflicted with his goals for his family. One day, in 2018, he called me and said, "Would you have a place in your company for me?" I responded with, "I am not going to recruit you, but if you want to come on board, then I know you will contribute." He did come on board, he contributed, and I made him an equity owner.

I struggled for some time when others would describe me as a visionary entrepreneur. It sounded pretentious because, to me, I could see opportunities and act on them, not realizing that only some have those giftings. What I realize now is that while it is a gift to be a visionary entrepreneur, that gift is pretty useless unless you have someone, multiple people in reality, who can embrace the vision and then create a replicable process to make it come to life. As we grew, we needed that integrator role filled, and Jarrin has excelled as our Chief Operating Officer.

In particular, I have so much appreciation for the way Jarrin has demonstrated Radical Integrity time and again. He has also encapsulated in his own words why it is so essential to our business, particularly regarding consistency as a crucial part of character-driven leadership:

Radical Integrity references consistency. Leadership is an important quality to live out, but it can be modeled in many different ways. Over the last several years of watching our business leaders, it has been their ability to consistently evaluate and adapt their style, focus, and leadership to the needs of the team and business that has enabled us to grow. This awareness of self speaks to a strength of character that is critical for a leader and business to not just survive but thrive.

In early 2020, it was our third son's turn to call me about working with us. Jennings had followed his older brother Joseph into the insurance world. He bought his own insurance agency at age 23 after graduating from Virginia Commonwealth University with a bachelor's degree in accounting. We often comment that his timing of selling his business in early 2020, just before the full impact of the pandemic, was impeccable. He provided invaluable input during the pandemic, sifting through various data points as they related to COVID-19 or as it involved economic trends. In a time of crisis, the truth of Proverbs 11:14 (NKJV) is borne out: "In the multitude of counselors there is safety." Having sons with wisdom and integrity to rely on was a huge blessing. Jennings has contributed by having a quick analytical mind, enabling him to review leases from a landlord or a marketing budget, and he has fully embraced our culture. Jennings has observed,

All the money, benefits, PTO, and so on in the world cannot create the deep-seated trust in leadership needed for employees to fully engage in the mission of a company. Only a consistent display of the willingness to do the right thing for the right reasons. People who are motivated by their trust and belief in their leaders give exponentially more than those who are only driven by money. From NIL partnerships to customers to employees, each person is willing to give more because of this deep trust, and the results are dramatically higher.

Jentry, in the number four spot in the family, was the first to step forward and become active in our company in 2017. He had received an insurance settlement after he was involved in a head-on collision with a car driven by an employee of a large Texas injury attorney. He called, looking for ways to invest the money. We had just expanded to our second location, yet still no bankers were willing to loan us money, so I was glad to have him invest as an equity owner. Jentry is the most inclined towards entrepreneurial pursuits out of all of our kids, yet he had another passion—becoming a police officer, which he pursued in 2016, eventually joining the Fort Worth Police Department. He is a natural connector with extroverted people skills that he has used in every work environment I have seen him in.

Kayla has also taken an interest in our business, and even with limited capacity due to her health, she used her love for basketball to connect us with multiple women's basketball players. Kayla has a unique perspective on how power is exercised in any realm. A lot of this is from her experiences with her health, lying on a hospital bed, and being subject to how someone uses their influence. She says:

> In businesses or any organization where the right character is not demonstrated by the leadership, there tends to be an abuse of both power and position. This abuse often occurs because people are not appreciated when the right character is not in play. Character is critical from the bottom to the top of an organization.

Our family has plenty of normal family issues, as you might expect. We are not perfect by any stretch, and at times, a lot of intense guys with the same DNA can be a little much for a conference room. Yet, it has been a great joy to have my family involved. My brother Joel even works for us as a contractor, installing our store decor in new stores prior to opening. We are as different as night and day, yet since he got all of the mechanical ability that was supposed to flow to me, it all works out. My oldest brother, Jim, also got involved at one point, and we relied on his expertise in technology to get us set up with our first CRM. Working with family is a huge life blessing.

The point of sharing those profiles of my children is first borne out of deep gratitude for the incredible blessing they are to me. But it also emphasizes a business point. Often, the culture of a family-owned business can be compromised because of family. Relationships can be contentious because you bring so much life history into the business, and every interaction has multiple overlays of historical events. Dad may be the owner, the boss, and the one who got mad when the son did not play a good game in Little League. The son or daughter may be the employee, the child, and the one who wrecked their dad's car when they were 16.

I spent the majority of my time before becoming an entrepreneur working in and around family-owned businesses. My longest tenure was over 13 years with Alexander's Mobility Services. When I joined them in 1994, their founder and president was Milt Hill, a charismatic and exceptionally gifted leader. In early 1996, he had outpatient knee surgery, and while recovering, he had a blood clot and passed away in his 50s. His son Donnie was only 28 at the time, and many people did not expect him to take over for his dad, given his age. But Milt did not raise an entitled son, but one who had worked his way up, first as a helper on the trucks, then as a driver, then overseeing quality assurance. Donnie had a dramatically different style than Milt, but he was authentic and shared the same genuine care for employees as his father.

He still leads Alexander's today, having overseen remarkable growth, and stands as an example of how family members can work closely together and reinforce a positive legacy.

I have known of other instances where there has been entitlement with a family member who is unqualified and is given a position, or standards are lowered with company policy not applying to people with the right last names. This undermines credibility and causes a lack of respect for the standards of character that the business is professing.

Altogether, our family experience has been about integrating the core principles of family and work. It has contributed to preparing them for life as working adults, teaching them invaluable skills that are hard to come by. To this day, it's why I suggest that other working parents do the same thing to whatever degree they can—and why I always advocate for keeping business and family life aligned as much as possible.

Finding Harmony and Alignment with Work and Family

One of the factors with the biggest potential to either hinder or accelerate business growth as it relates to character is family. While no family is perfect, committing to continue through good times and bad is essential.

My wife, Kathryn, and I have been married for almost 40 years. Like most people who spend that length of time together, there have been good times filled with harmony and blessing and tough times filled with relational and financial challenges as well as many other obstacles to overcome. We both would have thrown in the towel long ago had it not been for the grace of God in our lives, with an abiding belief that God designed marriage between a man and a woman to be a lifelong commitment and a source of stability for the family and our communities.

As I rewind the tape of almost four decades, I think of my parallel journeys of work and marriage and how they intertwined to create such blessings. For many, work competes with family in terms of the demands (and in some cases, family competes with work). There have been times that have been true for me, without a doubt, but overall, I have strived to make both aspects complementary in my life to everyone's benefit.

From my own experience, here are three ways to help create harmony between work and home—and you do not have to be married to apply them.

1) Introduce your family to your work world and vice versa. Share the reasons why you love what you do. When you get a chance, stop by work on your day off and introduce your family to your work buddies. For kids, this is especially powerful, as it will give them a positive connection to your working world. As I mentioned, I'm very proud that my kids grew up knowing my bosses, my coworkers, and even many of my customers.

2) Share your work goals with your family so everyone is aligned on the mission. If work is simply a selfish pursuit of our own interests, your family will resent it. If it is connected to a shared vision of being able to develop and grow personally, move to a better place, or provide an education for your kids, then it can be a joint effort. For the family members that can understand, explain what you are learning on the job and how it could help them, as well as the opportunities you have to make more money and how certain activities will either promote or prevent everyone's goals.

3) Work to maintain a healthy emotional balance. When things are going well at work, does your emotional state at home significantly change? If so, why? When we are emotionally mature, we can manage our victories and defeats in a way that creates predictability with our loved ones. They do not have to wonder if we had a good day to know whether we are going to be easy to

be with that evening or a challenge to live with. The same thing is true at work in that the inevitable personal challenges we all have should not create a roller coaster for our coworkers to handle.

In my experience, and hopefully many of yours, there are also friends who are close enough to be considered family. These relationships can also be either a catalyst for or a detraction from business growth.

If you have family or someone who you would describe as "family" in your business, or you are contemplating it in the future, consider the following:

1) Make sure that the family member is qualified to do the job. If you have difficulty being objective, ask someone else to interview them and give their assessment.
2) Are they "all in" on your culture? Are they willing to fully embrace your vision, mission, and values?
3) Can you hold them accountable even to the point of terminating them if necessary? No employee should ever be hired if they are exempt from these things.

Families working together can be a great blessing if they adhere to the same commitment to the vision, mission, and values of the company that any other member of the organization is expected to abide by. As I've learned, business and family should mutually support one another; they should not be at odds, whatever popular wisdom might suggest. With a faith and character-driven approach, it's possible to integrate them so everything works together and our relationships and interactions feel more connected. When we lack that connection or that connection suffers, that's when our lives can feel the hardest.

7

Developing a Culture of Care

Whoever wants to be a leader among you
must be your servant.
—*Matthew 20:26 (TLB)*

Care for people endures. Ken Blanchard shares the story that his friend, well-known pastor and author John Ortberg, told.

Let me ask you, who would you have bet your money on to last: the Roman Empire and the Roman army or a little Jewish rabbi and his twelve inexperienced followers? Isn't it interesting that all these years later, we are still naming our kids Matthew, James, Sarah, and Mary, and we call our dogs Nero and Ceasar? I rest my case.[9]

On a basic level, we must respect, care for, and appreciate the rich tapestry of differences in the human race and, ultimately, love them. When this is not forced or faked, it will show up authentically in every human interaction we have. In business, no human relationship is more important than the one we have with our employees. One primary indicator of company culture and the relationship between employer and employee is what happens to that relationship when it is tested by hardship and adversity.

Interestingly enough, the most lasting and abiding connections are often formed in times of deep adversity. As a child, I remember hearing my parents and their peers speak of growing up in the Depression, and while they discussed the hardships, they also had an affection for the experiences of those times. One of the meals that my dad and some of his peers most enjoyed later in life was pinto beans and cornbread, with the cornbread crumbled into a glass of milk or buttermilk and then eaten with a spoon. This was the most basic of all dinner menu choices, yet the taste seemed to be enhanced with the memories of overcoming the deprivation of the 1930s.

While it was not on the scale and degree that the Depression had for my parents and grandparents, experiencing COVID-19 and the pandemic was a time of significant uncertainty and fear at a very vulnerable time in our company's growth trajectory.

In May 2019, we opened our fourth store in Fairfax, Virginia, and then our fifth in Leesburg, Virginia, that November. Not long after, an opportunity came to purchase four stores in North Carolina, in Raleigh, Durham, Greensboro, and Winston-Salem, which we took over on February 1, 2020. That was followed by opening our Lynchburg, Virginia store in early March. From 3 to 10 stores in a year stresses a company even in peaceful and prosperous times. Then came the rumblings about COVID-19.

The first clue was when American Express reduced our credit limits almost overnight, even though we had always made our payments on time. They had more advanced warnings that significant trouble was brewing, and it was coming at a time when we were extended by growth more than at any other time in our history.

Crossroads in times like this are so significant for the culture of a company because it is here that every aspect of your collective character is tested. Suddenly, we had to make choices, do threat assessments around the well-being of our people, and then figure out how to survive in this environment. On March 16, 2020, we decided to close our stores, even though there had been no government mandate to do so yet.

Our business involves close, regular contact with our customers, and given the potential risk, we did not want to expose our employees to health risks that we could not measure. Initially, we thought it might be just a short-term closure, but after a few days, it was obvious that it would be longer. We were not in a position to pay employees to be at home, so we ended up having to furlough our store employees. That certainly didn't feel aligned with the way we wanted to care for our people, yet at the time, it seemed the best decision with the information we had.

Our store support center was much smaller than it is today, but those key employees were lifesavers. As referenced before, some offered to work for free, others volunteered to take pay cuts, and in Sarah's case, who was managing our payroll system, she proactively slashed her pay in the system before I could even talk to her about it. Then, they all got busy and began to work and collaborate like never before.

I named the group in the store support center Dragon Slayers, and we began strategizing on how to slay this dragon called the effects of COVID on retail and stay in business. While it seemed the rest of the world was binging on Netflix, the Dragon Slayers were working from early in the morning until late at night as we kept up with the latest government regulations and news, began exploring ways to create revenue streams as a 100 percent brick-and-mortar business, and began contacting customers to see if we could take orders by phone and mail them product. Laura was working closely with me as it seemed we had to develop a new playbook each day. Sarah helped our employees navigate through the state unemployment systems so they could get their paychecks as quickly as possible.

Katrina worked with me on scheduling out payments to suppliers to ensure we conserved cash. Grace and others in sales and marketing began hosting voluntary training and educational sessions on our collaborative platform, Workplace. Diane and Jennings explored the emerging government assistance programs. Jarrin, John, and Amanda hit the road as soon as possible to prepare to reopen. We were not fully back open for six weeks, and even then, sales were very meager at best. By late summer, the tide began to turn, and with the help of the Paycheck Protection Program and the fact that we had very little debt, we were able to pull through.

Recently, we celebrated Sarah's fifth anniversary with our company. She wanted to celebrate her anniversary with the Dragon Slayers, so we went to an upscale restaurant here in Richmond called Shagbark. As we worked through our various delectable courses of dinner, we talked about the memories from that time. Donna was hired just a week before we closed for the pandemic. Her comments were insightful as they pertain to employee care:

> When I was furloughed, I didn't know what the future held. I had always worked for larger big-box retailers, so I was expecting the same type of impersonal interaction. First, Sarah contacted me about wanting to help with my unemployment application. Since we closed before

the mandates came, and with her assistance, the employees were able to avoid the logjam that employees of other companies experienced. What I saw on Workplace was employees interacting with enthusiasm and energy, even in the middle of a pandemic. Finally, when I got a call from the executive team checking to see if I was okay, I said, This is the place I want to work for a long time.

As we finished dinner and left Shagbark, I felt a deep satisfaction. These were not just employees, but instead now close friends, tested by adversity and bonded by ties of deep character. Depressions, recessions, and pandemics are all things we would love to never experience. However, when you go through them with relationships like this, your life is infused with such a rich experience that it is impossible to truly measure the value.

This is an example of the multifaceted value of a culture of care for employees. It must be preeminent, and trying to maximize EBITDA at the expense of employee care is bad business, even in a pandemic. Business professionals across many fields recognize this truth.

When I met Kim Whitler, Senior Associate Professor of Business Administration at the University of Virginia Darden School of Business, I was impressed by her professionalism and intelligence. The more we have been able to interact, the more I have been equally impressed by the high standards she holds herself to, both personally and professionally. She invited us to participate in a case study on our approach to Name, Image, and Likeness in college athletics, which is founded on character. Later, she wrote an article for the Harvard Business Review that was published in the May/June 2024 print edition.

Concerning effective leadership at a company, particularly as it applies to executing a mission, this is what Kim had to say:

Principled leadership is the foundation of fair, equitable, and consistent treatment of employees, consumers, and other stakeholders. Having principles that guide actions is what eliminates destructive leadership behaviors such as: "Rules for thee, but not for me," "You scratch my back, and I'll scratch yours," and "In-group bias," where people prefer those most like themselves. Principles provide the "rules of the road" and steer leaders toward consistent and predictable treatment that creates a culture of fairness—something employees and consumers need to feel good about themselves and their relationship with the company and boss. As you look to leaders in business, government, media, and even education, we unfortunately see less and less principled leadership—core beliefs that guide a leader or company's behavior.

What I've taken Kim to mean by all this is that a company's leadership and culture have a major effect on how effectively it completes its mission. The vision and mission may "flow" from the top down, but it will not be achieved through the organization through punitive top-down mandates. It is not something that can be forced; it has to be willingly and enthusiastically embraced by everyone in a company. As Kim put it so eloquently, the leadership sets the tone for the culture of an organization, and then all of its members also bring their own motivations and ideas to the table.

Activating Care in Practical Business

Just as with any other aspect of culture, it is important to find ways to put it into practice rather than just talk about it. Of course, first, leaders need to model it, and it is very challenging to do it well. We then looked closely at our Vision, Mission, and Values to see what systems we could use to do this, and these were the main things we came up with:

Character and Servant Leadership: As we determined very early, our approach to instilling culture couldn't be just through executive mandates and top-down. Instead, it had to set a leading example and hold itself to the same standards we asked of others. To do this, we embraced the principles of character and servant leadership. In other words, our leaders are not "the boss" of the people they lead. Our leaders work for the employees and our customers to help improve their lives, all driven by their character and values. We decided to find ways to communicate this even in little things, like calling our offices Store Support Center instead of Corporate Headquarters. Our revenue is generated in the stores, so those of us in the office need the perspective that we are serving and supporting those in the stores. Dan Silverman, a very talented marketing and business executive, is a longtime friend and colleague whose perspective on this has deeply informed our own:

> The commonly held perception is that a leader who is of strong character is indicative of a positive trait. Yet, character, per se, is neither good nor bad. It stems from the Greek term kharakter, which is roughly defined as "to engrave upon or imprint on the soul." In and of itself, a leader's character can serve to construct or destruct with the most extreme impact on global civilization itself. So, its repercussions upon a mere company (and its stakeholders across the spectrum) can serve as a bona fide blessing that uplifts, inspires, and creates value. Or conversely, it can cause cataclysmic destruction and wretchedness. That's why the character of a business leader is important.

Reflecting on Dan's words, it's important to remember that everyone has character—whether good, bad, or somewhere in the middle. It is unavoidable, and without being intentional about it, it is easy to slip into practices we are not proud of. Servanthood is focused on serving others, not on serving oneself. Far too many good companies fall victim to self-serving leaders, but it's something that anyone can fall into without discipline. To avoid that, we've tried to build a culture of authenticity and self-reflection, reminding ourselves every day what we're doing and who we're really doing it for.

Employee-Centric Leadership: As the majority business owner and CEO, I constantly remind myself that leadership should serve our employees first. Our employees are our true "customers" in that sense; they are the people we need to think about and who we need to feel satisfied and fulfilled. I frame it this way because if we can lead in a way that satisfies our employees, it will trickle down to the customers they interact with, and everything will flow the way it needs to.

> *If you don't understand that you work for your mislabeled*
> *subordinates, then you know nothing of leadership.*
> *You know only tyranny.*
> —Dee Hock, retired CEO of Visa International

Someone who embraces employee-centric leadership is John Worden, one of my business partners and one of my best friends. He has the ability to truly listen to others and make connections with people everywhere, which has always amazed me. He came to us after being an owner of a Chick-fil-A franchise for 17 years. His thoughts on this approach to leadership have also had a great impact on me in life and business:

Those who take the risk to start or purchase a business, or those who accept a position of leadership in an organization, likely have a strong desire to succeed. A leader in a business setting should seek to make decisions that will ensure the strongest likelihood of success and positive impact on their organization. When setting a course toward success, leaders will have to choose the most important priorities for focus. Through various business cycles and over many years, priorities will certainly change. However, most seasoned leaders would affirm that at the top of that list of priorities, one significant priority should never change: A leader should endeavor to make very wise people decisions. S. Truett Cathy, the founder of Chick-fil-A and a mentor of mine, always said, "The secret ingredient at Chick-fil-A is the people." I would assert that the best way for leaders in a business to ensure the organization is infused with high character would be to hire strong leaders known for their high character exhibited consistently in their lives.

Whenever I think about our employees, I feel a sense of responsibility for them on a personal and professional level. If we are truly character-driven leaders, we will always want to take good care of our employees and will create systems to protect this value. This does not mean developing a culture where employees expect the employer to bail them out when they mismanage things. Rather, it is to be interested and active in responding when situations arise, both at work and elsewhere, that impact the employee. Ultimately, the lesson to stress here is simple: build the business around high-character employees, and the quality of the people they attract, both customers and other employees, will reflect that character.

Understanding the "Why": A significant part of a leader's job is to ensure that employees internalize the purpose of their work. This can be described as the "why" behind what a business does, and it is a key component of culture, job satisfaction, and success. As business leaders, one of the most meaningful things we can do is make sure our team has our "why" rooted deeply in their hearts and minds. Grace, a key member of our marketing team, understands the "why" and how it stems from leadership. Here's how she explains it:

> When individuals search for their careers, they often solely focus on the nature of the job itself. However, I've come to realize that while the work is crucial, it's equally important to have a boss who values not only the job but also the person that you are. This is something we should never underestimate. A boss who genuinely cares about you and your community can transform the concept of work from a burden into something you eagerly anticipate. Being part of an organization led by someone who genuinely cares about the well-being of others fills me with immense pride.

Character as a Driving Force in Business: Though we stress the importance of character in virtually every procedure and process we have, it's still worth mentioning again all on its own: if leaders inspire employees and employees drive the business, it's character that drives all of the above. The easiest way to see how important this is is to understand its opposite. My son, Joseph, who I've also been blessed to work with, puts it better than I could:

> The sad reality in today's world is that often, we do not know whom we can trust. Many people experience cynicism every day. This is no more apparent than in business. Many assume that greed is a deciding factor with each decision, that any "good deed" has a darker ulterior motive, or that every friendly smile will gladly stab you in the back when you are not looking. Sadly, there are good reasons for these presuppositions. That is why when you come across someone who defies those characteristics, it is truly inspiring. While skepticism would likely be present early on, a consistent honesty and authentic caring heart, shown day in and day out, will transform those around. Slowly, one

would see something different in this person, something that is not surface level. True character is devoted to those around them, showing selflessness that would convince the uncertain. It would inspire hope, spark a desire for excellence, and pull one to a belief in something bigger than themselves. This is the result of someone who lives every day with true character.

I also can't resist quoting our longest-serving employee, Katrina, here as well, since she has modeled high character since day one:

Character is the mental and moral qualities distinctive to an individual. All these qualities determine how we think, act, speak, and what we value. This then determines how we make decisions and the outcome of our lives. Every business leader has character, but it is vital that a business leader has the highest level of quality character. With this, they not only better those around them but also improve themselves in the process. It is important that the character we choose to have is the output we want to see and put into the world. Having a good character as a business leader ensures that the team you are leading not only admires the things you do but also values your input and, in turn, makes them want to have the same attributes.

Fostering a Culture of Care

Care should emanate from inside each of us, so self-care is critical before we attend to the needs of others. Setting the example ourselves will also help those who are coming along with us to prioritize this care in their own lives. Here are some of the habits I embrace to constantly strengthen my values:

Reading and Quiet Time: For me, I rely on a steady stream of reading and quiet time every day, which includes my Bible, other inspirational reading (in hard copy and on Audible), business books, and the occasional novel. I scan the Wall Street Journal and New York Times to catch up on headlines, but I try not to immerse myself in the news. Instead, this time is used to remove the mental clutter that may hinder me and renew my mind from the daily grind.

Exercise: Running is my time to process my stress and emotions and to get some good endorphins going. A friend once quoted his elderly father, who still runs in his mid-80s. His father said, "I have never said after a run, 'I wish I had not done that.'" I would say the same.

Connection: I have a close community, with friends and family playing key roles in keeping in close contact with me as we work through life together. This anchoring with a variety of people, from very young children to older friends from diverse backgrounds and varying educational and financial positions, is so important. It keeps me balanced, and I encourage this with our employees as well.

Speak the Truth in Love: When care, kindness, and love are present in the workplace, it is possible to have very candid conversations. I am not suggesting this is easy or that we do not struggle with implementing this key aspect of healthy relationships. Yet the ability to speak truth to ourselves and to others and to receive the same is foundational to having long-lasting developed relationships.

Celebration of Achievements: Finally, after working to implement the above day in and day out, it's important to celebrate ourselves for showing up and to mark each achievement as a milestone and a sign of the right action. It's something we've tried hard to do in our company, particularly because we pursue aggressive goals. After a record-breaking sales day, one of our employees, Darah, recently shared some words with the team that exemplified this concept:

We've been laying those bricks for over six months and piecing our perfect team together. We've laughed, sweated, and dreamed alongside one another— heck, we've even put furniture together with our own hands! We've defeated many obstacles to get here today, and we are only getting started. It has been said that a herculean task is best managed one task or step at a time, with great patience and focus. From here, we have to ask: How high is high? Because this is simply one more brick. We are so proud of you, team. We can't wait to see what we accomplish together next, and we are already looking toward our next minimum. Jonathan Cotten said to us not long ago: "The cavalry is coming! Be ready!" I think they've only just begun to show beyond the horizon. Brick by brick, my fellow champions, brick by brick.

Seeing these words makes me proud and very thankful for the progress we have made and the rewards that come over time from a culture of care.

Questions for Reflection:

As a leader, do you have structure for refreshment, calibration of your values, and honest input from those who know you, appreciate you and your contributions, yet also are not superficially impressed with you?

Can your employees quickly identify ways that the organization cares for them? This would be on an institutional level and on a personal level.

Does engaging in their work create more self-respect for employees, or do they feel demeaned or devalued through the process in any way?

Is there a conflict in the pursuit of profit, growth, or excellence with the care for employees?

8

Respect for People: Care for Customers and Everyone a Business Touches

Only those who respect others can be of real use to them.
—Albert Schweitzer, physician, theologian, and philosopher

The business of character, at its core, is loving people and respecting them. A healthy culture should deliver to the customers of a business a sense of deep value for who they are as individuals, not as targets for exploitation.

We are not in a transactional business. It is a business that you must put your heart and soul into because it has such a huge impact on our customers' lives. It is so fun to be involved in that culture. We know that if we are inspired to produce transformative outcomes for our customers, they will feel it. If we truly care and believe in what we're doing, the customer will feel it, too. It is an intangible thing to a degree, but it is the culmination of caring and how we express it through good hiring, effective training, and quality management. When a customer comes in and engages in that type of environment, they see that our business is something different. It is different from other businesses they normally interact with. Altogether, it is a different kind of place.

As mentioned, character takes time to build, and it often comes from experiences with family throughout childhood. In my case, my first memories of working were on our 70-acre farm in Crozet, Virginia. Saturdays were usually workdays, and if you were still too young to work, you were connected to it nonetheless by watching those who could. We had a beautiful home, and my dad made sure that the lawn and gardens were diligently cared for throughout the year. Having a construction business also provided a steady stream of people in our lives.

Looking back now, I can see the wealth of personalities of people who were involved in that work: carpenters, veterinarians, brick masons, painters, farmers, and college students who were yard hands all contributed in unique ways. Black, white, men, women, educated or illiterate, there was always something to learn from someone who did their work well. "Watch how he handles that shovel," Daddy would say. "See, when he throws that gravel, it always lands in the right place because he understands leverage? See that carpenter? Look at how his hands hold the hammer—he only has a thumb and two fingers, yet once he sets that nail, he rarely does anything other than drive it home in one or two licks. See Ike there?

He doesn't work at a furious pace, but he holds the same pace all day. When he's on the construction site, if there's a lull, he doesn't sit down—he finds something to do, like straightening a pile of 2x4s. And Cathy can transform that garden because she is relentless!"

Carl "Buddy" Horn and Kirt Kirtland were two UVA students who worked with us on weekends. They very patiently put up with me tagging along and "helping" them with their various work assignments. Not only did they work hard, but they modeled patience, diligence, and respect in a way that impacted me for life. In addition, having them take me to football games or the circus was a special treat and contributed greatly to my ability to connect and relate well to adults. Buddy went on to become an attorney and then a US Magistrate Judge, while Kirt started his own construction company and then went on to executive leadership in banking and finance. I like to think that those times doing menial labor together around our farm were positive experiences for us all.

The workplace was a critical classroom and was very helpful, given that I never understood some of the educational obstacles during my primary years in school. The classroom approach did not work for me, and if it were not for Mrs. Abel's intervention in the first grade, I might be illiterate today. She took me from struggling with sight recognition of words to teaching me phonics. It allowed me to make some good progress in reading, but other subjects did not come easy. Math, especially, was a challenge, as I struggled to stay focused. My typical trajectory through the school year was that things would start off well, but as time went on, I would get bored. The weather got warmer, the girls got prettier, and my grades went down the tube.

After quitting school in the ninth grade to do correspondence school, I worked during the day, came home, and did correspondence school at night. While my peers were attending conventional classes, pursuing organized sports, and mixing in the normal social activities, I was working on the farm and studying at night. As a result, my highest educational achievement was a diploma from the American School in Chicago, stating that I satisfied the requirements for a high school diploma. I had no class ranking, SAT scores, or college prep, but I did get an education—not in the typical academic sense but also in other ways that were even more important.

The education I received during this time was invaluable. I learned that the human body could work way past the point of saying, "I am really tired!" I learned that managing livestock is very tricky, and a lot of things can go wrong if expertise, diligence, and good fortune are not combined. I learned such valuable people lessons, including that the guy at the livestock auction with a wad of more money than I had ever seen was not my friend—he was a practiced scam artist who bought my cows at the gate only to run them through the auction at a higher price and pocket a nice sum without ever touching the animals. All of these experiences provided a tutorial on people and unconscious preparation for life.

The one exposure to business I really enjoyed was working with people, having worked alongside my dad at home shows and given people tours through model homes. Sales became the natural outlet, so I studied real estate and got my real estate license.

At 20 years old and just married, interest rates were at 15 percent, and I got to work. The story would be so cool if the next chapter were of me becoming a selling prodigy in real estate, following in the footsteps of my father's success as one of the leading real estate agents in his firm—but even though I learned some things and got some listings, less than a year later, Kathryn and I were struggling to make ends meet. Soon, an opportunity came along where I could earn a $15,000 a year salary working in sales for a moving company in Lynchburg, Virginia. That decision in 1985 set my course for the next 28 years in the relocation industry.

The company I went to work for was Young Moving and Storage, a black-owned family moving company, and I have always been thankful for the opportunity they extended to me. My initial role was residential sales and helping people plan their personal moves. After a few years in that capacity, I moved into corporate sales, where I approached some of the largest publicly traded companies in the US as a representative of a minority-owned business. These companies had publicly declared a commitment to minority business relationships, and I relentlessly pursued them for the fulfillment of their commitment.

What an incredible opportunity and an education it was to meet with and secure clients like McDonald's, General Motors, Marriott, Philip Morris, Frito-Lay, Pepsi-Cola, and so many others. Seeing their business decisions in action as they relocated managers and executives taught me many business and life lessons. Those early years taught me how to interact in professional selling environments. I got to see from the inside out how culture can vary from company to company. At McDonald's headquarters, for example, no one had a private office; the company's culture and purpose was to support the employees cooking french fries in the stores.

I didn't get into entrepreneurship until years later, but those early experiences forged my perspective and my approach, especially around how powerful respecting the wide range of people we encounter in life can truly be. I saw just how many different people a business could reach and how many stories—from both customers and employees— were intertwined in making things happen in a community. After a long career at different companies, when I did get around to purchasing The Good Feet Store and starting Easy Step Enterprises, I took all those lessons with me about how to treat other people—and how to create a culture with employee care as a foundation, then customer care, and then care for the community.

A quote I have loved for years on care for people comes from George Washington Carver:

> How far you go in life depends on your being tender with the young, compassionate with the aged, sympathetic with the striving, and tolerant of the weak and strong. Because someday in your life, you will have been all of these.

We have a framed poster of that quote in all of our stores and describe it as the Easy Step "people philosophy." Being "tender with young," whether work colleague, customer, or any other young person we may cross paths with, means having patience with those who do not have life experience. They will make rookie mistakes, so we need to work through that with them. The "aged," on the other hand, may have diminished strength or capacity in some way. Or they may struggle with technology, which I am hesitant to say since that puts me in that category.

The "striving" encompasses us all in one way or the other. The sick are striving to get well and the well are striving to stay healthy. The poor are striving to gain wealth, and the wealthy are striving to avoid becoming poor. Finally, "the weak and strong" evidence their need for care in different ways. I usually tell people that when I am feeling weak, I am likely easier to deal with. When I am feeling particularly strong, I need someone to come up behind me and whack me on the head to get a grip and come back to reality.

This quote is an example of how a principle or an idea can be extended into a business. In this case, we wanted to find a creative way to emphasize care for any and everyone. Wherever we intersect with people, there should not be a filtering of who deserves care or special treatment. If they are human beings, there is an opportunity to put this principle into action.

The focus of our teams on true customer care has helped boost our success. When our customers come in with a need, they experience

- a listening ear from our employees and teams
- professionals who apply their skills with caring competence
- positive results in the overwhelming percentage of cases
- holistic care that avoids the downside risk of pharmaceutical drugs, surgeries, or other invasive treatments

Training employees well is a way to show care for both the employee and the customer, yet it can often be tempting for executives to reduce costs and skimp on training. Joe Herlihy, president of Good Feet Worldwide, says, "Training is like mowing the lawn. It must be done consistently to be effective." Customers know when employees are well-prepared for their jobs, and skilled employees bring instant credibility to a business when the customers sense that the business values them enough to invest in how the employees care for them.

Getting these results involves everyone truly buying into our Vision, Mission, and Values. As we have grown, many people have dissected our processes and approaches to understand them and ensure they are creating the right results. As metrics and performance are studied, new approaches are developed, again with care to stay aligned with our culture. Once these new methods are integrated into the process, they have to be trained thoroughly and practiced consistently. This focus and discipline around details is not the purview of an action-oriented, ideas-driven entrepreneur. However, to achieve this entrepreneur's vision of a culture that cares for people, team members have to be brought on, empowered, and then properly left alone so we can live out this vision.

The advancements in technology, such as AI, have left many customers feeling disrespected by the impersonal and automated relationships many companies have with them. Gino Wickman, creator of the Entrepreneurial Operating System (EOS), references the phrase originally used by Isadore Sharp, founder of Four Seasons Hotel and Resorts: "Systemize the predictable, so you can humanize the exceptional." Humanizing the exceptional in customer care is a way to create a hedge against competition or hostile takeovers, as well-developed systems of customer care are not easy to imitate.

Clean Restrooms—A Practical Example of Care for Customers

Over the years, we've found proof again and again that investing in great customer experiences can produce a significant ROI even if it doesn't make a financial ROI in every single instance, and we work to ensure it happens in lots of small ways. A little example of this for us is having a sheet in every restroom for employees to sign off on after they clean it to verify that it's getting done. Those sheets are checked daily, which reinforces that we care for our employees by having a clean, comfortable working environment for them—but it is also a statement and influence on our customers and their purchasing decisions. After using the restroom, they often comment about the cute decorations and how clean it is.

Customers can tell mere moments after stepping into a retail store whether that company cares about them or is simply trying to sell them a product. We want our customers to sense just how much we care, both on a corporate and individual level. There are many things we do as a company and standards that we set for the express purpose of making the customers feel cared for. Of course, it's more valuable to hear from someone else—so the following is an account of a customer interaction one of my employees had:

Today, the final customer I had liked our system a lot, but found that it was something she really had to think about. She did not want to finance, as she was wary of having any credit. She ended up coming to the register with two pairs of socks, certain that was all she was going to purchase.

While I was ringing her up, she asked to use the bathrooms. When she returned from the back, she looked at me and said, "That is the most beautiful bathroom I have ever seen. I am going to purchase everything." I was honestly shocked. I asked her three times if she was serious, and she was. She talked to the employees in the back and told them that it was the bathrooms that convinced her to buy our system. She said she appreciated the cleanliness she saw in the little things, and it gave her a good indication of our intention to help people.

Two thoughts came to my mind after I read this account. The first was gratitude for having an unexpected reward for doing something that is simply the right thing to do, whether or not we get a reward from it. There is a proper sense of validation in seeing something we believe in (having a well-maintained restroom as an expression of a well-managed business) pay off. The second was the importance of making sure this type of experience wouldn't give us a false sense of hubris or smugness. The attitude had to be hard-wired rather than a result of external validation—because once that happens, introspection stops, openness to better or different ways ceases, and an unhealthy culture develops. Maintaining the humility and passion to always look for ways to improve while celebrating success is critical when it comes to operating a business known for treating its customers with character.

As we've learned firsthand, for a business to be character-driven, it must be about impactful customer relationships rather than mere transactions. This requires heartfelt commitment, and it must be rooted through at all levels, not cosmetic. Those core principles were drilled into me a long time ago.

Three Ways to Encourage Customer Care in Your Organization

1.   Find a creative way to express your "people" philosophy. It could be a quote, a graphic, or lyrics from a song. Capture the imagination of your team to make it real.
2.   Embed care into your processes and practice them. Care must be a reflexive response on the part of all team members.
3.   Make an insignificant business process an example of consistently applying this principle. Clean restrooms are not a cause for high performance, but they can be representative of the attitude behind high performance.

The business of character, at its core, is loving people and respecting them. A healthy culture should deliver to the customers of a business a sense of deep value for who they are as individuals, not as targets for exploitation.

9

Intentional Collaboration with Community Partners

July 8, 2016, is a day I will never forget. My youngest son, Jentry, was a rookie police officer, and he had started just a few weeks earlier patrolling a crime-ridden area in downtown Fort Worth, Texas, from 8:00 p.m. to 6:00 a.m. That morning, I woke up to hear the devastating news that five Dallas police officers had been killed the night before. It felt like an overpowering black cloud had enveloped me, and I stayed at home longer than normal, just trying to wrap my head around this news. Around 10:00 a.m., I got a call from the store saying there was someone who was waiting to see me. I quickly got ready and went into the store to find Andre, a former resident of the Richmond City Justice Center, who had been released and was working at a job on concrete floors all day.

His feet were killing him, and when he saw me, his face lit up. "I am here to take you up on your offer when you were teaching Jobs for Life at the jail," he said. We quickly got started on the fitting process, and as I put in his arch supports, I couldn't help noticing the ankle bracelet he had that was indicative of his parole. When Andre started to walk out with his arch supports and shoes, he gave me a huge bear hug and looked at me as if I had given him a million dollars. I reflected on the way that day started and prayed, "Thank you, Lord, for blessing me with a business that could be used to create such joy and reconciliation in a broken world."

Fast forward to May 13 and 14, 2023, and the Tent City event at Police Week in Washington, DC. Jentry flew out to be a part of it, and on Saturday night, he called me to tell me that the mother of one of the Dallas police officers who had been killed had visited the Good Feet booth and went through a demo. She loved the arch supports but was unprepared to make a purchase. He talked about it with our other leaders and decided to call and offer her a free Good Feet/Good Hearts 3-Step System of arch supports at no cost. She immediately started crying when he called her. "This is the best Mother's Day present I have received," she said.

What an honor it was to be able to engage with someone who had given so much and suffered so many days and nights of anguish. I am so blessed we were able to step beside her and help in a very meaningful way. Today, if we ever find ourselves struggling to identify a sufficient "why" for what we do, all we need is to reflect on moments like these to fill our cup of motivation.

Good Feet/Good Hearts

As a franchisee for The Good Feet Store, we have a program in place that allows each person who walks into one of our locations to walk out with a system of arch supports. Anyone who cannot afford to pay for the system upfront is able to apply for a financing program; if they are denied by that program, we have a secondary financing option available as well. If a customer applies for both programs and is denied, they automatically receive a 3-Step System free of charge. While this may seem like it would detract from our bottom line, I believe we are more than compensated for those free products by the tears of gratitude on the faces of those customers who urgently need our arch supports.

I was recently asked an interesting question by another business owner: "How do you all promote and market your philanthropy program?" My answer at first was very simple: "We don't as a major part of our marketing program. Internally, it is a great source of joy and inspiration, but I do not think we have ever discussed how to turn our program of providing arch supports to those in need into a marketing program." After discussing it more, I began to reflect on whether we could share the program externally in a limited way, though I knew we could only do it if we could find a way not to appear self-serving.

As I mulled over this idea, it again reinforced the idea that our purpose was not just to maximize sales and profits. Some people perceive business as a ruthless machine, endangering anything that would diminish the profit-making ability (sadly, this is too often the case). However, if we see business as something that can be redeemed and leveraged to achieve outcomes with multiple good effects, then we do not have to seek a profit ROI on every activity. When we help lift another person's load or show care to an individual who can't pay us back, the inspiration from those events provides the ROI.

Repeatedly, I see so many of my employees demonstrating those same ideals. They give up their time or commission to help someone, and I can tell that those moments lift their hearts as much as the stellar sales days. Now, please do not misunderstand: we stay in business because we watch our metrics and seek to perform every day at an exceptionally high level. But I think it is worth noting that this success can then give us that much more ability to make a difference quietly yet profoundly in people's lives.

The following is just one example of a testimony from a salesperson talking about a recipient of our Good Feet/Good Hearts program:

> Ms. Betsy has been suffering from nerve damage in her feet and ankles since the age of 17. She has had 18 surgeries on both of her feet and is still in pain. Ms. Betsy actually cried as soon as she stood up in her supports. She said it had been so many years since she felt that kind of relief. We tested the strengthener, and as we finished the walk in her maintainer and returned to the booth, I noticed her son wiping tears from his eyes. It totally broke my heart to see her cry tears of joy as she left the store with her free Three-Step System of arch supports.

Community Partnership at Easy Step Enterprises

When you have a foundation of employees who are engaged and character-driven, the impact can spread outward into your local community as well in a variety of ways. This is the second major part of having a community-wide impact. Some of them happen somewhat naturally, but others involve more active engagement and direction from the leadership. There are a handful of principles we follow to make sure this happens in the right way:

- Community Engagement: Taking care of employees makes care for the customer a natural next step. Once that happens, you truly unlock the ability to make a community-wide impact because your employees take ownership of it. Our employees get so inspired when they can help others, whether helping someone who was incarcerated reintegrate into the work environment or walking alongside people who are grieving the loss of loved ones in the military. There are many ways to encourage your employees to play an active role in their communities, which in turn creates a sense of motivation that is impossible to duplicate through speeches or slide show presentations.
- Business as a Community Pillar: Many businesses and business models have a negative net effect. They may sell something and make money, but the way they operate creates drag on the overall community—by creating health problems or other dependencies, for example. Our model is something different. After purchasing our products, our customers often come back and say things like, "This was the best purchase I ever made. This has changed my life." Beyond that, the impact we make on our customers gives us the ability to reinvest in our community, which I would encourage all business owners and entrepreneurs to do. In this way, a purpose-driven business can be a treasured institution in a community, providing true career opportunities rather than just subsistence-living jobs. These kinds of businesses provide positive, community-oriented benefits that uplift customers as well.
- Reinvesting in Community Partnerships: Partnering with people doing great work in your community adds another level of inspiration to your employees. They will see that not only do they have a good job and a

respectful work environment where they can truly help customers, but they can also move the meter with larger scale problems as well. Currently, Easy Step is involved with several nonprofit organizations. We refer to them as Community Partners because the folks at these organizations are able to be the hands and feet that help others with specific areas of need.

Many people can write a check, which we do as much as we can, but building relationships is the most rewarding way to build community. Through our Community Partners, Easy Step now has employees who are learning what mentorship truly means. It means visiting with a family member in their community at a housing project through our partnership with Strategies to Elevate People-STEP RVA. It means seeing the gratitude on a family's face when they pay tribute to their fallen military family member in front of thousands during Military Appreciation Night honoring TAPS family members at the Richmond Flying Squirrels. It means learning more about the unique challenges of kids with intellectual disabilities and their families through the wonderful work of Jill's House. In all the above, these are people who often have had no one in their corner until these nonprofit organizations came along. We are blessed beyond measure to have a retail business that allows us to not only support these groups financially but to walk alongside them in their work.

Choosing Community Partners: Easy Step Enterprises' Partnership with TAPS

To partner with the right organizations, business leaders need to do their due diligence and ensure that their Community Partners live up to their own standards and that each is aligned with the company's Vision, Mission, and Values. We have processes in place to make sure we do this successfully, but one of the best examples of a successful partnership for us has been with TAPS, headed by Bonnie Carroll.

I first met Bonnie Carroll in the fall of 2008. William Chatfield, Director of the Selective Service under President George W. Bush, introduced us, and I was immediately drawn to her passion and commitment to serving the families of fallen military members. Bonnie's husband, Brigadier General Thomas Carroll of the Alaskan National Guard, died in a plane crash in 1992. In her grief, she found that there were significant support and assistance gaps for those grieving the loss of loved ones in the military. With that motivation, she formed the Tragedy Assistance Program for Survivors in 1994.

I will never forget the conversation Bonnie and I had on December 31, 2008, when I called to express my desire to work more closely with her organization in 2009. Her immediate response was reflective of the way Bonnie immerses herself in her mission of serving those who are in deep grief and need. "If you want to help, I have someone with a need right now that I'm trying to address," she said. The case was a young widow of a member of the Texas National Guard who had served in Bosnia but had recently died by suicide. The widow was not a US citizen, did not have access to many resources, and was facing eviction along with her infant child.

We began to strategize, and through a friend of the family, I was able to arrange for a temporary home for the woman and her child for a few weeks. We then connected her to an immigration attorney who was able to help with some legal paperwork that would allow her better access to resources. It was the start of one of the most inspiring and fulfilling relationships in my professional career.

Bonnie's work at TAPS aligned with my vision for Easy Step for the following reasons:

1. Their mission is crystal clear, and they pursue it with a single-minded focus and dedication. Bonnie's leadership is central to this clarity, and many anecdotes of her servant leadership abound. I once visited with a TAPS family member who recounted her first call to the TAPS 24-hour helpline. She called around 2:00 a.m. and was expecting to get a recorded message. Instead, she was greeted by a live person who handled her call with tenderness and compassion. It was only later that she learned that the person who answered her call was none other than Bonnie Carroll herself.

2. TAPS exercises fiscal discipline and carefully stewards their donations. An annual budget of $13M is equivalent to the marketing budget of comparable organizations. Great work is accomplished by having lean administrative overhead, with all employees active in their mission and expert coordination of a strong volunteer base. We saw this commitment to fiscal stewardship on prominent display in February of 2022 when Russia invaded Ukraine. TAPS's affiliate organization, TAPS International, had formed a chapter in Ukraine at the request of the US State Department after the Russian invasion of Crimea in 2014.

    In an effort to raise maximum support for the victims of war, Bonnie declared that donations to TAPS Ukraine would go 100 percent to Ukrainians who were suffering. We were able to partner with TAPS and Samaritan's Purse to deliver winter socks to Dnipro, Ukraine, at a time when logistics were difficult and the need was great. Later, we were able to fund two ambulances, complete with our logo, to operate on the front lines. When a donor can see a direct link from their donations to the end recipient, it provides confidence in the fiscal integrity of the organization.

Given the centrality of our culture to our long-term success, we seek strong alignment between our values and those of our community partners. Although our vision, mission, and values are not explicitly Christian, they are founded on Biblical principles. James 1:27 says, "Religion that God our Father accepts as pure and faultless is this: to look after orphans and widows in their distress and to keep oneself from being polluted by the world." TAPS and our other Community Partners provide a conduit to fulfill our own mission-related vision. This changes the entire construct of the relationship, from a charitable donor donating to a needy nonprofit to the structure of a company investing in a well-managed charitable entity. This, in turn, provides multiple moments of inspiration and a reshaping of our purpose.

We have consistent opportunities to engage in direct contact with our community partner recipients. Our many experiences connecting with TAPS family members have been life-changing for so many in our company. Linda Ambard captivated our employees at an Annual Team Meeting as she recounted losing her husband Phil to a terrorist attack in 2011 when an Afghan colonel whom he was mentoring turned on him, taking Phil's life and the lives of seven other servicemen. Linda had a lifelong passion for running and planned to use the 2013 Boston Marathon as a milestone of progress in processing her grief. She wound up being a block away from the terrorist attack there, which added another layer of trauma to her story. To date, Linda has completed 220 full marathons on all seven continents.

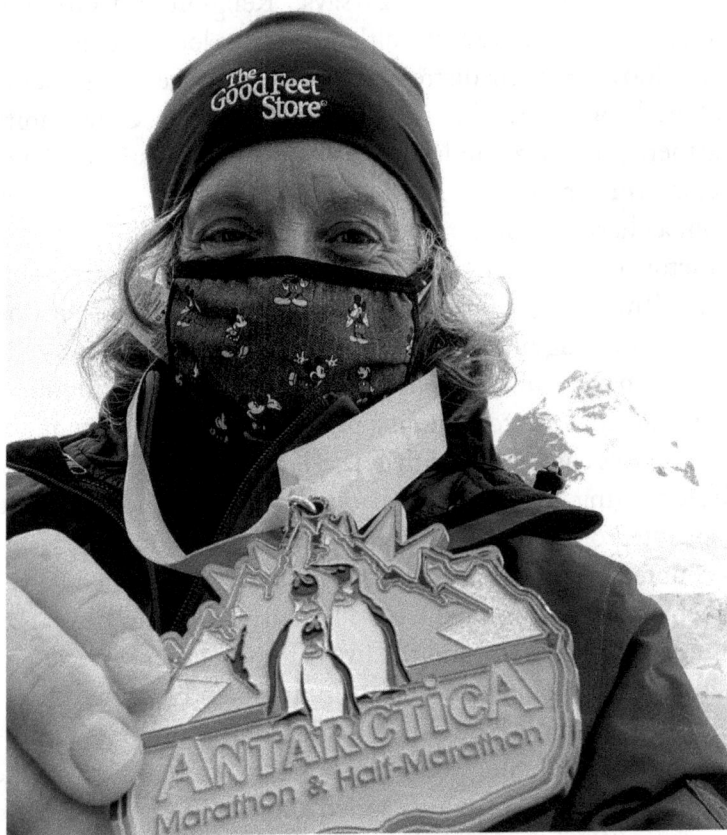

We were thankful to be able to sponsor her Antarctica marathon, where she proudly displayed our logo at the South Pole. If you are interested in reading more about Linda's story, her book, *Courageously Alive—A Walk Through Military Loss*, is available for purchase on Amazon.

Whether it is the spoken accounts of heartbreaking stories as Linda shares or the unspoken ones seen in the eyes of TAPS widows, children, and other loved ones who are left behind, the effect has been to produce thankfulness in our hearts. Our sacrifices and support are not the story, even though at every event we host, these dear families are profuse with their thanks. When you consider their sacrifice, pain, and loss, which came from a mutual commitment to serve our country, working with purpose takes on new meaning. Working to lift others up, to "walk beside people on their journey, regardless of their journey, because we are people who love our neighbors," this part of the vision statement no longer exists as a hazy thought but rather an integral part of why we are in business.

Bonnie Carroll and TAPS are part of the wealth-building benefits of the entrepreneurial journey. Even if I had $100 million to give away, I could not have the rich and varied experiences of engaging through a business with these community partners. These relationships help answer that searching question that inevitably comes to many entrepreneurs and business people: "What did we really accomplish? What difference did we make?" When I started my entrepreneurial journey in 2014, one of my commitments was to form relationships with organizations like TAPS. Their structure and missional integrity would serve as a model for others in the nonprofit space that we would partner with over subsequent years.

Customers, Community, and Advocacy

Community Partnerships can be incredibly rewarding for everyone on all sides. Facing the hard things in life takes an emotional toll on even the most prepared of those engaged in community service. We love the opportunity to engage with them, encourage them, and demonstrably show our support.

One of my favorite weeks is Nurse Appreciation Week, where we pack and pass out gift baskets in each of our markets to nurses who go above and beyond to care for their patients. Again, the impact of a person of character can be difficult to explain and impossible to put a price tag on. These are the people who have to deal with emotions of extreme pain and extreme joy each day. They see the miracle of birth and the agony of death.

Despite the feeling that our times have a monopoly on depravity, the truth is that evil has been around for a very long time; now, we have simply mastered the ability to export evil in vivid detail to every corner of the globe. But how have people throughout history endured war, economic depression, disease, hunger, and all the other ills that mankind wrestles with? How did they do it while raising families who endure and who are still thankful for their memories?

None of us were wired to enjoy prosperity and good times for sustained periods of time. When we go for stretches in this state, we do not have the seasoning that adversity pro- duces, and we become weak and shallow. However, becoming consumed with tragedy or hardship does not allow us to refresh our minds. This is why it is so important to get out of our bubbles and help others as much as we can, as well as to properly enjoy the blessings we have. Investing in our Community Partners is not due to having to apologize for success or feel bad about enjoying things. They can both be held in balance. My friend Wayne Jacobsen says, "To survive the brutalities of this age, we also have to celebrate the joys life offers. We get to hold those things in tension." Doing this means reflecting on the immense sacrifices others have made for us, thanking those who have served, extending a helpful hand to others, and enjoying the life and health we have with immense gratitude at the same time.

Reflections and Exercises

Understanding "Why": When looking to make an impact in the community, it's important for business leaders to be selective about who they work with and how. While every community has non-profits working in the community, they don't all approach their work the same way. Not all of them know how to run a business up to acceptable standards or character and values, and not all of them are transparent in using the money they bring in for all the right purposes. To this end, it helps to ask:

1. Does the organization have a clear sense of "why" for their activities? Are they already making a significant contribution that you could add to, or is their leadership less impactful than it could be?
2. How does the organization's "why" line up with your company's "why"? In principle, are you aligned in terms of vision, mission, and values?

Defining Vision/Outcomes: Based on the framework of mission, values, and vision, it helps to co-define what the ideal outcomes would be for a successful collaboration. To that end, companies should consider:

1. How does your candidate for Community Partnership run their organization? Are they as committed to their values and mission as they say they are, or are there inefficiencies? Where are they most effective? Are there other organizations that accomplish the same things better?
2. How aligned is the organization with your company? If there are differences in your vision, mission, and values, are there still enough opportunities for a productive partnership?

Defining Supporting Policies: Building off both of the above, whatever productive alignment exists will need to be supported by processes and systems to keep everyone accountable. With this in mind, it helps to consider:

1. *What tweaks to daily/weekly processes will go in place to make these partnerships successful? What needs to happen, what metrics will be used, and how will success be measured? What responsibilities and roles will each respective organization "own," and is everyone equally committed and accountable?*

• • •

While one of the great benefits of a character-driven business is the impact it can have on a local community, it isn't something that happens automatically. Truly character-driven businesses are about greater principles: communal welfare, social bonds, love, and respect. Once these pieces are in place, a business can focus on true, sustainable growth in a well-adjusted way—one that always begins by leading with character.

10

The Competitive Stage: Can a Business of Character Compete in the Marketplace

Let your light so shine before men, that they may see
your good works and glorify your Father in heaven.
—*Matthew 5:16 (NKJV)*

As much as we talk about compassion for others, community building, and having a purposeful culture, the reality of business is the enterprise has to be competitive and viable in the marketplace. I have seen two different types of responses to business and growth, with both having their respective downsides. The first is fear of growth, and the second is a traditional competitive approach. This latter approach is often framed as a win-lose approach, where in order to win, you have to "take" from someone else. Without shying away from reality, there's an element of truth to that: moving into a new market and successfully controlling it could be considered "taking" a win from someone else on one level. But if we look at it through the lens of character-driven competition to provide better outcomes for others—and not as a way to add notches to our belts or boost our egos—then we can embrace competition without any ethical ambiguity.

A healthy sense of strategy, competition, and operational excellence is what drives businesses to grow and makes the world a better place, but successful growth requires careful self-reflection in our decision-making. It can be a challenge, but it's a worthwhile pursuit. Both fear and an unhealthy attitude to competition have to be addressed.

On February 7, 2018, I woke up in Carlsbad, California, where John Worden, one of my best friends and coworkers, and I would be attending a meeting at the franchisor headquarters. I was facing a major life decision: whether or not to purchase another franchisee's store in Rockville, MD, and enter the DC market. The price was right, but the challenge of taking on a major market with all the associated high costs of advertising and other expenses was daunting. Our store support team consisted of John and two other employees, one of whom was a recently hired marketing person, with a small team keeping things rolling in the Richmond store. Our location in Newport News was starting its third month.

That morning, I went for a run on the beach and took a quick swim in the chilly Pacific. Then, I opened my Bible for my daily reading. The passage of the day was the parable of the talents. In this story, Jesus shares how three men had been given talents, or bags of gold, based on their abilities to invest for their master. The first one received five bags and invested wisely, getting five more bags in return. The second received two bags, invested those, and received two bags in return. The last one received one bag and then buried his money for fear of losing it. When the master returned, he commended the first two for their diligence and faithfulness. Then, he turned to the third and asked why he had buried his money. "Well," responded the third servant, "I knew you were a hard master, so I went and buried my money because I was afraid to lose it." The master rebuked this servant for his fear and cast him out.

After reading this account, I had my answer: fear was not going to dominate us. I was not going to bury my talents. Instead, I would invest them—but for the glory of God, not simply to fuel my own ambition. As an organization, we didn't know how we would approach this huge challenge, but we planned to take it one step at a time and wait for the answers. The answers came in time, with the right people and the right processes, though, of course, we made missteps along the way. Initially, we did not have the money we needed. I made the agreement with the franchise owner for the Rockville, MD store, and a few days later, the president of Good Feet Worldwide at the time, Matt Coleman, called.

"Is there anything we can do to help in this venture?" he asked.

"Buying media in the DC market is very expensive, with only one store to allocate it to. I am just trying to figure that out," I responded.

"How about we just reimburse you for the purchase price of the store," were the next words that came out of his mouth.

I was stunned and incredibly grateful. In light of the current environment, that is unbelievable—today, the cost of acquiring the DC market would be a multi-million-dollar acquisition! Sometimes, timing in business is everything, and it was certainly the right time here. We still had to fund our advertising and development costs, but this first win was a huge answer to our prayers and got us going.

Fear is one of the biggest obstacles we can face as we tackle challenges and pursue goals, and it is one of the spiritual blocks that get in the way of a character-driven approach to developing strategy in business. It is often based on some real elements, but then it takes on a composite size and form that is irrational. For business leaders, I would encourage you to ask yourself: is fear stopping you? Are you playing it safe and burying your talents? These questions are not about being more reckless but about recognizing what we have all been given by God and then maximizing those gifts. My question of "How can we do this?" that I asked on February 7, 2018, has since been answered—and in large part, it happened by filling in the faces of our now over 250 employees.

My encouragement to other business leaders is along the same lines: while still being motivated from the right place, lean into your fears and don't shy away from taking appropriate risks for the right reasons. If you can understand your fears, you can turn those obstacles into part of your strategic plan. Do not let your fears deny you some of the greatest blessings of life.

When you think about growing a business and simultaneously keeping your character and culture intact, it is essential to have a healthy perspective on strategic competition. One thing that has been most inspiring through the years is seeing competition and collaboration within, between, and from our store support staff at each of the stores as we have pursued excellence every day. It spurred my thinking on the difference between healthy competitors vs. unhealthy competitors. Consider the contrast between these two expressions of competition:

Testing Character in Competition

Healthy Competitors	Unhealthy Competitors
Compare against our own potential.	Compare exclusively against the opposition.
Want strong opponents since a strong opponent sharpens our own skills.	Desire weak opponents to inflate the ego.
Are satisfied in knowing the best effort and execution was put forth.	Are never satisfied, regardless of the money, the victories, or the achievements.
View awards and recognition as simply a scorecard of executing a great plan, team chemistry, and how many people were helped.	Find identity exclusively in awards and medals.
Always seek to reinvent themselves (Apple, FedEx, 3M).	Rely on past victories (AOL, Blockbuster Video, GE).

Have an abundance mentality and seek to enrich and lift up customers, employees, their community, and others in their space.	Measure everything in zero-sum terms, where a victory for one is an automatic loss for others. If management/ownership wins, then employees lose. If a salesperson wins, they defeat a customer. If one entity wins, then it signals a loss for another entity.
Are fun, kind, and invigorating.	Are mean-spirited, arrogant, and exhausting.
Can attach one chapter of success to another since the path to victory was balanced, respectful, and ethical.	Primarily achieve one-hit wonders since they are driven in an unbalanced, envious, and self-centered way.
Are willing to share keys to success to inspire and help others.	Only share keys to success if it exalts them and garners more "likes."
Can handle both victory and defeat with grace because they have developed internal wholeness.	Are condescending in victory and resentful in defeat.

Work to understand the difference between these attitudes. As you consider your competitors, retain a healthy mindset. When you're winning, celebrate—but do not let it build cockiness or complacency. If we are not yet winning, we have to remember the progress we've made since we started rather than focus on the distance of how far we still have to go.

• • •

When it comes to business growth, the discussion often centers on all the potential upside. If we're not careful, it can lead us to an overly rosy view of reality—and it can make us lose touch with what life is really like for the people in our communities. When this happens, we can tip over into pure profit-seeking instead of approaching competition and business growth from a grounded and healthy perspective.

As the challenges of business continue, I sense a real degree of collective weariness in society. Although the years 2020 through 2022 were stressful, it seems that we are consistently facing one obstacle or another. Adversity impacts everyone differently in degree—but everyone feels some impact. In terms of viewing environmental conditions and economic difficulties realistically and applying that to character-driven business growth, here are some practices and insights I like to keep in mind:

Take time each day for a period of reflection with gratitude. Negativity and anxiety are like a tornado that forms in our minds and gradually spins with more and more velocity. To fight against that trend, we have to remember what we do have with a sense of gratitude. If you are in great health, give thanks for that. If you have enough money to cover your expenses and a little left over, then say thanks—especially considering the reality that so many people in the world are trying to function at a minimal level of income. If your life has a relative amount of peace and calm, think about those around the world who have to face the possibility of a massive army invading their country. Many things can make the gratitude list if we pause to count them. By making gratitude a foundational practice, you can turn any situation around very quickly.

Control the things you can control. My friend Benjamin Harris emphasizes that we all have a circle of concern and a circle of influence. We can be concerned about things that are happening thousands of miles away and pray about those, but what about the things we can control? Some of these things include a healthy lifestyle, a budget for our personal finances, and investing time in things that count. While this isn't an excuse to isolate yourself or become selfish, it's a reminder to keep a sense of balance. After thinking about all the problems of the world and starting to feel powerless or overwhelmed, take a second to refocus your perspective. There are things you can control right now, and it is still your duty to turn your attention to them.

Maintain a personal development plan. Read, learn, grow, and then rinse and repeat. Do not wait for the perfect external conditions to achieve your goals because that day will never come. Instead, do it now! Even if you're stuck at home due to illness, don't use that as an excuse to write off the precious time you have. Again, change your perspective: perhaps you've been given a gift to slow down, prepare, and learn something in a calm and concentrated way.

In January 2014, I did not know what the future held. Then again, in March 2020, I did not know what the future held. Today, our focus on developing a high-character culture throughout our organization has paid off, and we are enjoying a level of success that would have been hard to conceive of when I first opened the store or during that 2020-2022 timespan. As a result of that, I thank God for His grace and blessing, especially during those difficult times. When times get tough, what helped us most was to remember to live out our Vision, Mission, and Values.

Putting all of this together, my perspective on business growth is simple: we need to redefine our unexamined assumptions about profit and competition to bring them into the realm of a character-aligned life. We can dispel the "win at all costs" mentality in favor of something more strategic and value-driven—a more nourishing, faith-based, and community-oriented approach to what is often a cutthroat topic. With these core elements in place, you may be surprised to find growth starting to take care of itself.

11

Building a Network with Character

Two are better than one,
because they have a good reward for their labor.
—*Ecclesiastes 4:9*

The business of character is not a solo endeavor. It takes developing relationships with others who share your values, principles, and goals in both business and life. Few things are more harmful than aligning with someone who seems to align on those things yet disappoints or even betrays the relationship. Other people are so critical to not only success but also enjoyment along the way. A strong network and powerful, healthy relationships are essential ingredients.

One of the greatest struggles that I have had to overcome, and that I have observed in others with relationships and networking, is dealing with the perceived and real imbalances between people. We like to have connections with people where we relate with them in an even or balanced relationship, and not where there is an uneven structure. When there is a big difference in life experience, finances, age, gender, race, education, or status, it can feel uncomfortable or mismatched, especially when we feel we are in an inferior or weaker position. We all desire significance, and imbalance in the relationship can feel very uncomfortable. I think back on the days on the playground and being on a see-saw with someone bigger. The feeling of being powerless, with your feet dangling in the air, at the mercy of a heavier person, is not fun. If they had bully tendencies and decided to bounce you off, then that was even worse. Resolving these feelings and conquering the fears we all have in these relationships is critical to developing a dynamic network.

Like many things in life, building a network is not that complicated, and it is something that anyone can practice. It all comes down to using a relational cheat code: Be interested versus striving to be interesting.

We show interest in other people by asking questions, letting them talk, and then truly listening. As I have interacted with celebrities, top business leaders, and those occupying positions of power, the best relational equalizer is to be interested. Be interested in them as people, their families, and their interests. Once, I had lunch with a former NFL player and current media figure. We spent our lunchtime talking about a number of things but very little about football.

As we got to the end of our time, I asked, "How can I help you?"

He paused for a moment, looked at me, and said, "No one ever asks me that question."

Then, we went on to discuss his interest in engaging with underserved communities.

Have a relational goal; be interested in people. Ask great questions and listen. For me, this requires great discipline to do well because it is so easy to talk, especially if I feel pressure. Yet, asking questions removes relational pressure and is one of the most powerful forms of emotionally connecting with anyone.

When we think of networking, don't confine it to the influential or those we believe can help us. I go back to the summer of 2016 when I first became connected to the Richmond Justice Center's REAL Life (Recovery from Everyday Addictive Lifestyles) program. Dr. Sarah Scarborough started this program to address the needs of incarcerated inmates struggling with addictions. It was a fantastic experience to leave my cell phone in the car, walk into that jail, and follow the deputy up to the pod where 10–15 inmates would be waiting. Usually, two or three of us volunteers would be involved, and we spent the time mentoring these men.

During that summer of heightened racial tensions and interactions with the police, one particular night, we concluded our time in prayer as was the standard practice. We stood in a circle, with two of us in street clothes and a group of men in orange jumpsuits.

I asked, "Could I make a prayer request?"

"Sure," responded the men.

"It is for my son," I said.

"Absolutely."

"He is a rookie police officer in Fort Worth, Texas," I said.

One of the inmates led off in prayer. "Heavenly Father, we pray for Jentry tonight. Keep him safe, Lord, and help him to do his job." That inmate in an orange jumpsuit will never know how much he contributed to my life that night.

That helped develop within me the aspect of character of not restricting who can impact me in my life and vice versa. When our network is full of a wide spectrum of people, we will have consistent contributions from many perspectives.

Networking should be a character development process, just like any other activity in business. Yet, if we approach it as a fishing expedition instead of a human connection endeavor, it falls short of its potential. When we can connect well with a wide range of people, from the country club to the jail, we exhibit integrated character. It is enriching to learn about the hard lives that some people have, and it can help us to have empathy and a greater understanding of people. I have listened to many stories of people's lives where abuse, hunger, neglect, and abandonment were commonplace. The countless memories I have of sharing a meal with family around a dinner table were like a fairy tale to many of them. It is valuable to have those people in your network because they will dramatically alter your worldview.

Another joy of having a wide network is reconnecting with people whom I have not talked to in many years. Recently, an employee sent me an email saying that an old friend, Tim Lehigh, had stopped by the store to say hello. Tim and I worked together at a farm in Ivy, Virginia, just outside of Charlottesville, in 1981, though we had lost contact. He left his number, and we got to catch up later that evening by phone. Now, 41 years since we worked together, Tim is 69 years old, still works on Malvern Farm, lives in the same house, and has five children and 14 grandchildren. He bought the farm manager's house that he lived in when I worked there and has continued caring for the estate of the wealthy family who still owns the farm (with the original owner's children and their grandchildren).

Those reconnections in our networks can also be good reminders of certain aspects of good character we might not see often. After my visit with Tim, I reflected on how much

I respected him. He had always been an example of faithfulness. He was true to his upbringing in Lancaster County, Pennsylvania—of caring for the animals, the land, and his responsibilities as if he were the owner. He has been rewarded over the years by having a beautiful place to raise his kids without the burden of being an owner. But importantly, keeping a job for 41 years is not something many people do these days. He is a living example of someone applying the correct principles of character. Given his position, he could easily cheat the owners out of money or waste their resources since he does most of his work while no one is looking. He has always operated with the utmost integrity and still does. Keep on, Tim—more people are watching than you realize.

Overcoming Self-Limitations in Networking

Over the years, one thing I've noticed is that networking can be an intimidating prospect for a lot of people, even if they bring a lot to the table in terms of value and character. Being around others' successes can sometimes make us feel uncertain of ourselves or less accomplished. In these cases, it's important to take a step back. Are we operating by our own principles day in and day out in our lives and businesses? Are we positively impacting the people in our communities? If so, we should be able to present ourselves with heads held high in any room we walk into. If we are clear in our own consciences, we should be able to see through any internal doubts or limitations we may be placing on ourselves.

From my own experience being in rooms of people who could have intimidated me, I've learned four key lessons that stand out. With these in mind, anyone should be able to navigate any room they walk into with confidence and integrity.

Don't Be Intimidated: Though we can all feel intimidated in the presence of highly successful or powerful people, I'll never forget what someone once said to me about visitors to the Oval Office: "They are lions in the waiting room and lambs in the office." On one level, it means that someone's bark is often a lot worse than their bite—but on another level, it also means we need to be respectful of people's time and agency. Show up to networking events prepared, ask thoughtful questions, and show interest in others for who they are as people, not just what their position is or what they've accomplished. As a general rule, highly successful people dislike people fawning over them or being tongue-tied. Instead, be natural and genuinely engage with others.

Be Kind: "What is desired in a man is kindness." Kindness works both with the rich and powerful and with the weak and vulnerable. When we show the same attitude to both categories of people, we reveal our own integrated character. Kindness is showing genuine interest in people and in their stories, and thoughtful questions are a great way to express that kindness.

Protect People: Whether very successful or still striving, all of us need to guard ourselves against exploitation. We tend to think that exploitation only happens to the weak, but celebrities or high-profile individuals are often subject to exploitation as well when people use information about them to garner attention or status for themselves. As such, whenever you're given private access to influential people, be very scrupulous about what you share. Trust will be gained when they do not worry about being exploited. We also should afford the same dignity and respect to someone who is lower profile. Before we share the story that someone has shared with us in confidence, maybe of experiencing violence or extreme deprivation, have we checked to get their approval before sharing their story? They may be comfortable sharing with us, but they may not be comfortable with their story being shared on a broader level. This is basic respect for human beings.

Find Ways to Give: Balance in any relationship is crucial. Often, when we feel intimidated by someone, it is because there is a lack of balance between us. We feel we are stuck on the high end of that see-saw with our feet dangling. Finding ways to give that are appropriate for the relationship and context is a way to bring those exchanges back into balance. It communicates that we feel power as well, even if there is a differential, rather than taking a "They have it all, what can I possibly offer" type of attitude.

Grow through Outreach: Finally, making these changes does involve a learning curve, and it won't all happen overnight. Even so, it also won't happen simply by thinking differently and not taking action. It's crucial to remember, even if it sounds familiar or clichéd, that growth happens *outside* our zone of comfort, not inside it. Staying in the storage room of stores or behind a computer all day is a guarantee that we won't grow our networks in the way we want to. Instead, we need to reach out to others and create opportunities to foster new connections. True relational growth is cultivated through deeply rooted confidence and character, which means proactively taking on challenges and overcoming them.

Relationship Lessons to Grow Your Network

Often, we think of building a network as something we have to start on from scratch or as a process of adding a bunch of "new" things to our lives to make up for a lack of some kind. Though there's certainly a benefit to having new experiences and opening new doors, we often under-appreciate what we already have when it comes to developing a strong network. If we look at our lives more closely, we can often find that we have all the ingredients for a strong network already; it's simply up to us to take advantage of those resources. In my own life, I've seen this play out time and time again in a few different ways.

The Influence of Unique Individuals: In 2022, I attended a memorial service for a man named Bobby Hull, who was a friend of the family for many years and married my cousin, Laura. Bobby loved his family dearly and was one of those "break the mold" types of people who felt comfortable in his own skin and did not worry about doing things in a different way. He was an entrepreneur who did everything—from selling old whiskey barrels turned into furniture, Corvettes, and tires to operating a dump truck, all before finally retiring in his late 40s. When I was 17, he even almost convinced me to buy a '55 Thunderbird and restore it as a project. That would not have ended well, as he failed to appreciate that I did not share in his mechanical aptitude. Still, it was Bobby's own version of diligence that had the greatest impact on me to this day in business.

In the '80s, Bobby had a tire store in Charlottesville, Team Tires. At that time, tire stores or auto repair shops were often not the most well-maintained places and were often covered in dirt and grease. Team Tires was different. The shop was kept neat and orderly, and the bathroom was particularly spotless. When you walked into the bathroom, it was always meticulously clean and brightly decorated. To me, it was an important lesson that creating a network is not just about *who* you are but also the *what* and *how*—what kind of environment you create or associate with and the processes you have in place to maintain your standards.

When we started our business, that was a value we embraced as a result of Bobby's influence. In the early days, when we just had the Richmond store, Bobby would often stop in with his encouraging smile. He will be missed, but we are thankful for the memories he left us with and the encouragement. To this day, his life and impact remind me of a quote from George Washington Carver:

> "When you can do the common things of life in an uncommon way, you will command the attention of the world."

A Biblical Lesson on Business and Networking: As an entrepreneur, it has never been my goal to "command the attention of the world." It has, however, been a goal to set the highest standards for myself and my company through the people we interact with—especially when it comes to character. Sarah Rogers has been a faithful employee since 2018, and she is one of the first people to interact with our new employees when they are introduced to our company because of her great heart for others. The following is one of her favorite Bible passages, Luke 16:1-13, that relates to business:

Jesus told his disciples: "There was a rich man whose manager was accused of wasting his possessions. So he called him in and asked him, 'What is this I hear about you? Give an account of your management, because you cannot be manager any longer.'

"The manager said to himself, 'What shall I do now? My master is taking away my job. I'm not strong enough to dig, and I'm ashamed to beg— I know what I'll do so that, when I lose my job here, people will welcome me into their houses.'

"So he called in each one of his master's debtors. He asked the first, 'How much do you owe my master?'

"'Nine hundred gallons of olive oil,' he replied.

"The manager told him, 'Take your bill, sit down quickly, and make it four hundred and fifty.'

"Then he asked the second, 'And how much do you owe?'

"'A thousand bushels of wheat,' he replied.

"He told him, 'Take your bill and make it eight hundred.'

"The master commended the dishonest manager because he had acted shrewdly. For the people of this world are more shrewd in dealing with their own kind than are the people of the light. I tell you, use worldly wealth to gain friends for yourselves, so that when it is gone, you will be welcomed into eternal dwellings.

"Whoever can be trusted with very little can also be trusted with much, and whoever is dishonest with very little will also be dishonest with much. So if you have not been trustworthy in handling worldly wealth, who will trust you with true riches? And if you have not been trustworthy with someone else's property, who will give you property of your own?

"No one can serve two masters. Either you will hate the one and love the other, or you will be devoted to the one and despise the other. You cannot serve both God and money."

There are many good commentaries on this passage, but for me, this one from John Piper sums it up well:

Here's the basic point: Don't worry about being a shrewd investor in this age, where you can provide a future that will only fail. Instead, be a really shrewd investor by investing in people's lives. Use your resources to do as much good as you can for the glory of God and the eternal good of others—others who will go before you and welcome you home.[10]

Well said, Sarah, and a great template for being in the business of character.

12

The Tie That Binds: Achieving Diversity and Harmony with the Business of Character

In today's polarized society, a reasonable question would be whether it is possible to have a distinct culture that also attracts and unifies diverse employee and customer groups. This is a hot topic among the very largest corporations today and also in small businesses. Often, it seems the strategy is simply to not offend anyone, which ironically can sometimes then turn into offending almost everyone. The mistake, it seems, is an effort to project something or erect a façade rather than just being who you are. In other words, be in the business of character. If you have nothing to hide, and there is a constant effort to maintain integrated character, being authentic can be refreshing.

As a young person, I only knew Doug Williams as most football fans know him: a quarterback for the Tampa Bay Buccaneers who led them to the NFC Championship and then later with the Washington Redskins, as quarterback and Super Bowl XXII MVP. Once again, being in business facilitated the opportunity to engage with him as an endorser for The Good Feet Store. As we got to know each other better, I learned about the incredible backstory of his life.

Doug Williams is not just a Super Bowl champion but also a civil rights leader, breaking down the barrier for other black quarterbacks and players. He endured the slurs and taunts of fans, being the lowest-paid starting quarterback in the league while at Tampa Bay, yet retains a positive and hopeful disposition as he engages with people, with no traces of bitterness. He introduced us to the Black College Hall of Fame, which is connected to the Pro Football Hall of Fame, and we continue to engage with them as a sponsor. I have learned so much during these experiences about the experiences of black people and the struggle against racism.

These and other experiences and relationships have helped us develop several principles that have guided us in our journey and impacted our culture, our diversity, and our collective character.

1) **Safe and respectful.** In our vision statement, we state that we want to provide "A safe, respectful environment, full of opportunity, for anyone willing to embrace our mission and values." The prerequisite for employees is simply a willingness to embrace our mission and values. A "safe, respectful environment full of opportunity" covers a lot of territory. This means that there needs to

be intentionality on the part of leaders to address things that have historically created barriers in the workplace.

In the summer of 2020, we were not only dealing with the effects of COVID-19 but the significant unrest due to the death of George Floyd and the resulting protests. Donna was a new store manager in our Winston-Salem location, and one day, a middle-aged woman came in and purchased a 3-Step System. The next day, she returned, wanting to return it. As Donna was trying to help and resolve the situation, the woman threatened to call her son to "handle things." Soon after, her son, a young man in his mid-20s, came to the store and started to behave aggressively. He was clearly very angry about the transaction. He demanded that she get a complete refund or he would call the sheriff, and he also stated that he was an employee of the third largest bank.

Donna has won our Unwavering Positivity Annual Award because she has a perpetual smile, unbounded energy, and a can-do attitude. She has served in multiple retail locations, from fast-food to military exchange locations to big-box department stores. As a woman of color, working for multiple decades in the South, she has also had to learn how to handle both implicit and explicit instances of racism with poise and grace. In this case, she politely handled the return and then notified the executive team out of concern that the customer may raise the issue again. She did not expect any action on our part.

When I heard about this incident, my blood pressure rose. I knew how much Donna and all of our team members were giving on a day-to-day basis, and I felt that this customer had crossed the line of a "safe and respectful environment." I asked for the son's contact number and called him.

Me: "Hi, this is Jonathan Cotten, the president and owner of the store you visited with your mom on Saturday. I understand that an issue that you were concerned about came up."

Customer: "Oh, yes, we got it all squared away. I appreciate your call, but everything is fine."

Me: "I understand that the transaction was taken care of, but our employee felt very disturbed by your threat to call the sheriff and your reference to working for a major bank."

Customer: "Oh, I was just worked up and didn't mean anything by it."

Me: "I understand that you were worked up. I just feel some follow-up is needed with our employee. I would propose two options. The first would be a simple email to Donna with an apology for the interaction. That would mean a lot to her and to me since she is a highly valued employee. An alternative option would be for me to contact the executive offices in Charlotte and allow them to be the arbiter in the situation and prescribe a resolution."

The customer quickly agreed to write the email and issued an apology. In this situation, protecting the employee was paramount, even at the risk of offending an individual customer. I was totally fine if this situation went viral because I believed the court of public opinion was squarely on our side.

2) **Adversity produces diversity.** Overcoming adversity is often one of the best ways to develop character. While I am a white male raised in a loving, comfortable home, I have experienced adversity, and those times have challenged me and developed my character. However, when I compare the challenges of my life to some that others have faced, it creates deep respect for their journey. When you are at a disadvantage due to your race, gender, ethnic background, disability, or any other factor, it often requires using high emotional intelligence to succeed. Leveraging position or the support of a majority alliance is not available. The cliché of "he was born on third base and thought he hit a triple" contains a lot of truth in certain situations. Consider the difference between two fictitious applicants who, when asked to share the story of overcoming adversity, these are their respective responses:

Applicant #1: "In my junior year of high school, we had a great tennis team. We felt we were destined for a championship, but our star player was injured. We got bounced in the quarterfinals. I always felt we should have won, and it took a long time to process that."

Applicant #2: "I always felt self-conscious growing up. I was raised by a single mom, and often, in middle and high school, I was hungry or felt I didn't have clothes that fit right. I knew I had to earn respect in the classroom by being super-prepared, and on the basketball team, I was focused on lifting everyone up. It worked, and I continue to apply those principles today."

While that is a fictional account, it is not far from the real cases I have been involved in. Athar is from Pakistan, and he and his family fled from that country due to the Taliban. I really cannot relate to the challenges he has faced, but the adversity in his life has created a deep well of character that he draws from as he works with coworkers and customers. Here are his comments about using adversity to propel you forward rather than allow it to slow you down.

After spending 30 years in the hospitality industry, I've transitioned into my first sales role at Easy Step Enterprises. While the industries differ, my background has instilled in me a profound understanding of client and coworker needs. My experiences have taught me the value of empathy, active listening, and tailored support. My past experiences have been a source of strength and perspective, teaching me resilience, empathy, and the value of inclusivity. These lessons have helped me build strong relationships with coworkers and customers and have shaped my approach to work and life.

I feel incredibly fortunate to be part of Easy Step's environment and culture, which values inclusivity, support, and growth. This aligns with my own beliefs and has made me feel a deep sense of belonging.

Despite my unique background, I've adjusted seamlessly to the company culture thanks to the welcoming team. My experiences have broadened my perspective, enabling me to contribute to the team's diversity and growth.

Absolutely, I feel safe and respected at Easy Step. The company's commitment to inclusivity and support creates a sense of security, allowing me to be my authentic self and share my thoughts and ideas freely.

3) **Broaden your circle.** A test of the character of a company and its culture is to get the perspective of people outside of your immediate circle. Connect with people other than family members, long-term friends, and neighbors; engage with people from different backgrounds. Having people in my network of friends with diverse backgrounds is a way to test the wholeness and completeness of my personal character and the character of our company.

Benjamin Harris is an example. We first met in jail. Neither of us was an inmate, but we participated as volunteers in teaching Jobs for Life at the Richmond City Justice Center. Benjamin is a few years older than me, and when he was a child, Richmond was still very segregated. His mom worked for a restaurant in the city, and when they were not busy, she could only wait on black customers. When they got busy, they would have her wait on customers of all races. Sometimes, she would only receive a nickel or dime tip from white patrons.

She would come home and share these stories with Benjamin, which, when combined with other experiences that he had with white people, created a deep-seated hatred in him towards white people. As a teenager, he joined the junior Black Panthers and was later involved in an armed robbery of a grocery store with some other guys. He was convicted and given a prison sentence, and in his words, "I just saw a white policeman, a white prosecutor, a white judge, a white jury, and white prison guards. I hated all white people."

He went to prison, where he converted to Islam. He vowed not to speak to any white people, which caused him to be put in solitary confinement. One day, while praying toward Meccah, he heard a voice say, "Believe in my son Jesus." He associated Christianity with a white man's religion, so initially, he ignored this message. But he could never get away from it. One day, he got down on his knees and asked Jesus to forgive his sins, including his hatred for white people.

Benjamin and I are close friends now, even though our initial point of significant connection came at a time of deep racial division in America. As fellow business owners, we have connected on work matters, and then Benjamin invited me to his church every month to have a Reconciliation Sunday service. We have shared these Sunday services with a joint message for the last four years. Connecting to Benjamin and his congregation has provided great insight into how various issues are viewed differently in diverse communities. While I can still struggle with having the depth of empathy needed to be an effective leader, this connection is a tremendous benefit on multiple levels.

4) **Prioritize care for people over politics.** Authentic care for people is a unifying force. When people see a culture that extends care for people without discriminating criteria in any way, it will produce confidence. I find great biblical support for this in Galatians 5:22-23 (NLT), one of the most well-known passages of the Bible: "The Holy Spirit produces this kind of fruit in our lives: love, joy, peace, patience, kindness, goodness, faithfulness, gentleness, and self-control. There is no law against these things!"

These truths provide an excellent template for how to engage internally and externally with people. Having a safe working environment, engaging with all employees with respect, and creating equal opportunity are cohesive initiatives. Respecting all customers, even those who do not have adequate financial resources, creates a consistent response that an entire organization can embrace. Being selective about who we roll out the red carpet for is eradicated.

The same is true for connecting with the community. For example, our work with TAPS as a community partner has had this unifying effect. Regardless of someone's opinion on the government, our military, or the advisability of various military engagements in the past, caring for the victims of war is a unifying activity. "There is no law against these things."

Authentic diversity is essential in a healthy company and the business of character. Yet, it should not be contrived or reactive to the day's hot topic. When employees, customers, or the community sense a façade with no real substantive commitment to these issues in the organization, there will often be a backlash, and some-times, it can be significant.

Consider the following questions as you reflect on your organization:

- Do employees feel you genuinely care for them and the community they are most attached to?
- Are any incidents involving a breach of safety, dis-respect, or a challenge to opportunity for employees dealt with consistently and unequivocally?
- When people engage with our company, do they see people that look like them?
- Does the organization's outreach to the commu-nity provide opportunities for all employees to engage in?

Having a diverse workforce, working with diverse cus-tomer groups, and coming alongside others who do not look like me and have radically different experiences than mine has been a tremendous blessing to me. These experiences are humbling, inspiring, and educational; they give tremendous depth to my life and our entire company.

13

The Road Ahead

As I think about the next phase of life, the future has many unknowns. Our world looks pretty fragile from many different perspectives. Yet, just as living by faith each day has brought us through this far, the same approach will carry us through the challenges of the future.

I plan to stay active in business and continue to grow and learn. There is dynamism in the marketplace, which is fun and provides a unique place of connection and influence. I want to encourage others of faith and conviction to maintain relevance and viability. Our world needs to see enduring values lived out in practical ways rather than being relegated to the theoretical.

Staying active is my plan because health is a gift from God that needs to be maximized. In the thousands of miles I have run, thankfully, I have never twisted an ankle, sprained a knee, or had any other significant injury. I can't take credit for that because I would not be described as a methodical trainer. It is just another gift that I feel a responsibility to manage well—to be a blessing and not a burden to others.

A motivation for staying active and healthy is now having 13 grandchildren. Their world is very different from when I grew up in Crozet, Virginia, 50+ years ago. Their world is substantially different than their parents' world. I don't want to be the doddering granddad sitting in his rocker and smoking his pipe. (I guess pipes are not a thing anymore, but you get the point.)

I love jumping on the trampoline with them, wrestling, swimming, and hiking with them. As I learn more about horses, I want them to grow in their love for horses and animals, as they have that interest. We recently all went to Utah, near Zion National Park, to celebrate Kathryn and me being married for 40 years and my 60th birthday. What fun we had swimming in the pool of the magnificent house we rented, hiking the paths in the majestic park, and talking with them about their various interests! From Grayson, the oldest, to June, the youngest, they all educate me and help me grow.

Growth in business looks a lot different now with 280 employees than it did 10 years ago with two or three employees. It requires a lot of thought to understand how to let go of things that others can do so much better than me while not abdicating the proper place of influence I should have. Insecurity, fear, and reacting instead of responding can still be in the mix just as they were years ago because just as I had never run a business in 2014 with one location and three employees, I haven't run the kind of business we have now, with 42 locations and 280 employees and growing. It requires humility to "stand down" and let others stand up, take on challenges, and celebrate their victories. The meeting is going on in the conference room, and not only were you not invited, but you don't even know what the subject is. What if they kill something that you prize? What if they launch something you think is inadvisable? What if they make a decision without getting your input? As a rule, we have a good structure for how our business flows, but I would be dishonest if I said that these thoughts or feelings sometimes do not arise. A different kind of growth is needed.

Today, I am experiencing more and more of what Dan Sullivan describes as the Four Entrepreneurial Freedoms: freedom of time, freedom of money, freedom of relationship, and freedom of purpose. I find immense joy and gratitude in enjoying these four freedoms. I also feel a deep sense of responsibility, particularly as it relates to that last freedom— freedom of purpose. What is my purpose, and am I staying true to that purpose?

Kayla recently had an accident where she fell at a basketball arena and had to be hospitalized for five days. She could have been much more seriously injured or worse, but being with her in the hospital once again reframed my purpose. Seeing her suffering with pain, witnessing the devotion and care of the nurses, and being so frustrated with the breakdown in communication in a healthcare system—all brought me full circle to reflect on our journey. While I have had so many experiences that have inspired me, have met so many people, and have been blessed with overall incredible health over the last 10 years, her life has been filled with pain, disability, and a shrinking social circle. This is the injustice of life, so when we succeed in any arena, we need a massive infusion of humility. Why do some of us receive what feels like ongoing rewards while others deal with unimaginable adversity? God knows that answer, and in his time, he may reveal it. For now, we should never forget both sides of that continuum and the people it represents.

As I think about the path ahead, here are the questions and goals that come to my mind. Take a moment and write down your own.

1. What is the Business of Character at this point on our journey? Is it sales records, financial status, or impressive growth? Or is it taking a God-given opportunity and prayerfully, thoughtfully maximizing every opportunity for impact? We can still take an interest in our employees' lives and search for ways to develop, encourage, and support them. We can make sure that our value proposition for our customers is strong. When we get legitimate input on a gap that a customer sees or feels, we still respond as quickly as in the old days, when our survival was measured by success with a customer one at a time. In every community we are in, we find an incredible opportunity to nimbly and yet substantially come alongside those who are valiantly engaged in nonprofit work and moving mountains. Are we still involved in those ways?

2. One of the realizations I have had as a Christian is that God does not call me to success but to faithfulness. Jesus said, "As much as you have done it to the least of these, you have done it to me (Matthew 25:40). What is in our wake as we achieve goals? Is it exploiting others, particularly the vulnerable, or is it simultaneously blessing others along the way? Are we maximizing the opportunity each day to strengthen relationships through the influence of our business, or are we waiting to arrive on the mystical "Someday Isle" (someday I'll help, I'll give, I'll lift up)? The accomplishments, money, and awards will all be gone one day, and the only thing remaining will be the lasting relational impact of what we did. What are we leaving in our wake?

3. For me, the point of sharing my story and the collective story of those who have been involved is that it will be an inspiration to others. What kind of inspiration and to what end? I hope the simple phrase "work/life" can be reexamined so that work is not on the negative side of that equation. Instead, work and business are positive energy sources that infuse purpose into other areas of our lives. Does work drain you or supply you with energy? I am not proposing some panacea that work is not difficult or energy-depleting at times, but overall, are Monday mornings a dreaded day on the calendar or a time of enthusiastically rising to meet the opportunities of another week? I believe they can be the latter, and I always want to find new challenges that sharpen and inspire me.

The Business of Character is for me, as a leader, to regularly practice self-reflection, to commune with my God, to invite truth-tellers into my life, and to continue growing. I want to always remember that the true heroes of business may never have an impressive title or position, and their work of opening doors for others at a hotel, framing walls on a construction site, or repairing an aircraft engine are all activities with incredible significance and value.

Above all else, I want to emblazon the words of Jesus on my mind, "And what do you benefit if you gain the whole world but lose your own soul" (Mark 8:36, NLT). To me, this can be applied in multiple ways. The most important application, and the primary one, is not to replace an eternal relationship with Jesus Christ by chasing money and temporary success. He offers forgiveness and life today and for eternity. I also believe that someone can "lose their soul," as in forgetting for a time what the lasting things in life are, even if they are Christians, and pursue cotton candy achievements that taste good for a moment but leave a deep hunger for the most enduring and satisfying things. This is one of the most dangerous traps of business and a siren song that has entrapped many otherwise successful people. What are those potentially detrimental tradeoffs or compromises that we make? When should we say "yes" to a proposal or give an unequivocal "no" if it crosses clear lines of values and our established character?

The marketplace still has a hunger for the Business of Character. It is a differentiator, a magnet for talent with character, and a powerful retention tool for customers. One of the greatest benefits is that if we end each day with the conviction that we have pursued the Business of Character with authenticity and integrity, we can put our heads on our pillows each night with the belief that our work was well done.

Conclusion

Being in business has been a great blessing in my life and that of my family. My passion is that my work would be a ministry that blesses many. My prayer is that this book reflects that desire and achieves that goal. I am incredibly grateful for the opportunities and the measure of success we have had. When I soberly consider all that has happened, I can see how just a few different circumstances or decisions could have created a very different outcome. What we have is really a tremendous resource to be carefully stewarded, and as long as we are working, my prayer is that we will humbly stay in the Business of Character.

As I have shared my story, my prayer is also that you will receive it as simply an account of lessons learned, both positive and negative, from which you can benefit. As I stated earlier, for sheer financial success, many other stories would exceed this one. What I hope to convey is the joy we have experienced along the way.

I am thankful to serve a loving God, to have a devoted wife of more than 40 years, to be surrounded by a beautiful family, and to have the many relationships that being in business has facilitated. Many of the concepts and principles we follow in our business are the compilation of insights from others. I hope that to the degree that you have found useful items in the preceding pages, you will likewise cut, paste, and apply them in your sphere of influence.

To God be the glory, great things He has done.

Jonathan Cotten
September 2024

Endnotes

1   US Bureau of Labor Statistics. n.d. "Business Employment
    Dynamics: Entrepreneurship and the US Economy." Accessed
    November 11, 2024. https://www.bls.gov/bdm/entrepreneurship/
    bdm_chart3.htm.

2   NBCNews, Mae Anderson, and Michael Liedtke. "Hubris—and
    late fees—doomed Blockbuster." Aired September 23, 2010.
    https://www.nbcnews.com/id/wbna39332696.

3   Cox, Lindsay K. 2024. "32 Vision and Mission Statement
    Examples That Will Inspire Your Buyers. HubSpot Blog.
    Accessed July 7, 2024. https://blog.hubspot.com/marketing/
    inspiring-company-mission-statements.

4   Warby Parker. n.d. "History." Accessed February 5, 2025.
    https://www.warbyparker.com/history.

5   Chick-fil-A. n.d. "Our Culture and Values." Accessed February
    5, 2025. https://www.chick-fil-a.com/careers/culture.

6   TED. n.d. "Our Mission: Spread Ideas, Foster Community and Create Impact." Accessed February 5, 2025. https://www.ted.com/about/our-organization.

7   Warby Parker. 2022. "Impact Report: Executive Summary." https://www.warbyparker.com/assets/img/impact-report/Impact-Report-2022-Executive-Summary.pdf.

8   Taken from Day by Day with Charles Swindoll by Charles R. Swindoll. Copyright © 2000 by Charles R. Swindoll, Inc. Used by permission of Thomas Nelson. www.thomasnelson.com. https://insight.org/resources/daily-devotional/individual/act-medium1.

9   Blanchard, Kenneth, Phil Hodges, and Phyllis Hendry. Lead Like Jesus Revisited: Lessons from the Greatest Leadership Role Model of All Time. Nashville, TN: Thomas Nelson, 2016.

10   Piper, John. "Does Jesus Commend Dishonesty in Luke 16?" Desiring God, 1273. November 7, 2018. https://www.desiringgod.org/interviews/does-jesus-commend-dishonesty-in-luke-16.

Acknowledgments

To my wife of 40 years, Kathryn. That evening in April of 1982 is still riveted in my mind. That's when I saw this gorgeous girl holding her niece, Molly, with such tender affection. Marrying you as soon as possible became a goal, and that goal turned into a reality on June 3, 1984. What a journey it has been. We have had exhilarating moments and the relational, mountain-top experiences, then the devastating moments when life hands you the blow-out tire moments on the cold, lonely stretches of the highway. You believed in me 40 years ago, you believed in me throughout my career, and at a pivotal moment, as I was contemplating jumping into the world of entrepreneurship, you believed in me again. Without you, there would not be this book. You prefer the quiet places, the service behind the scenes, and I love you for all that you are and the way you have encouraged and anchored me through the years.

To my exceptional sons, Joseph, Jarrin, Jennings, and Jentry. We have had such incredible times together, loving, laughing, crying, sweating, playing, and, yes, a lot of work. My goal was to teach you, encourage you, be present with you, and love you. In turn, you have loved and encouraged me, and now I learn so much from watching you move in and out of your roles as godly men—as husbands, fathers, businessmen, and leaders.

To Kayla, my warrior. No doubt, as the youngest child and the only girl, you have received some special favors. Yet, when measured against the incredible adversity life has dealt you over the last 12 years, everything pales in comparison. The countless hours we have spent together, in hospitals, beside your bed at home, and having spirited debates about things we see differently have changed me forever. As I have tried to view the world through your eyes, it has filled me with such purpose to look out for those whose lives are filled with challenges. NEGU: Never Ever Give Up! I love you girl!

To Laura, my assistant and coworker, without whose help this book would have never been possible. You created the first draft of this book, compiling writings from my emails. That was an amazing selfless gift that still impacts me today. Thank you for being a person of impeccable high character and for bringing to life things that, at one point, were just a distant dream.

To the many Easy Step employees whom I am unable to name individually, having you in our company has been one of the most amazing blessings in my life. This is the real treasure of being in business: experiencing what it means to live relationship-rich. Thank you for changing my life, the lives of your coworkers and countless customers, and for creating a beacon of hope in our communities.

About the Author

After more than 25 years in corporate sales, in 2014, Jonathan became a business owner when he purchased The Good Feet Store in Richmond, Virginia. Two years earlier he had been introduced to the Good Feet system as a customer and became a believer in the system when it relieved his pain from plantar fasciitis.

The Good Feet arch supports helped him so much that he ran his first marathon that year. The following year, he returned to the store raving to the owner about how much he loved the product. The owner looked at him and asked, "You wanna buy the place?"

He did, and he has since added stores from Cleveland, Ohio, to Destin, Florida, and from Nashville, Tennessee, to Baltimore, Maryland. This journey has inspired many by demonstrating a business's power in its relationships with employees, customers, and the broader community when it is in the "business of character."

CONNECT WITH JONATHAN

Follow him on your favorite social media platforms today.

www.ingramcontent.com/pod-product-compliance
Lightning Source LLC
Chambersburg PA
CBHW071603210326
41597CB00019B/3385

* 9 7 8 1 6 3 6 8 0 4 2 4 8 *